Monsters of the deep
SOCIAL DISSOLUTION
IN SHAKESPEARE'S TRAGEDIES

David Margolies

Manchester University Press
Manchester and New York

distributed exclusively in the USA and Canada by St. Martin's Press

Copyright © David Margolies 1992

Published by Manchester University Press
Oxford Road, Manchester M13 9NR, UK
and Room 400, 175 Fifth Avenue, New York, NY 10010, USA

Distributed exclusively in the USA and Canada by
St. Martin's Press, Inc., 175 Fifth Avenue, New York, NY 10010, USA

British Library Cataloguing-in-Publication Data
A catalogue record for this book is available from the British Library

Library of Congress Cataloging-in-Publication Data applied for

Paperback edition published 1994
ISBN 0 7190 3441 8 *paperback*

Typeset by J&L Composition Ltd, Filey, North Yorkshire
Printed in Great Britain
by Biddles Ltd, Guildford and King's Lynn

CONTENTS

PREFACE

Like countless schoolchildren, I was at an early age inoculated against Shakespeare. When the plays were offered in school as something 'good for you', I knew I could expect more pain than pleasure and was generally successful in avoiding them. Then having pursued for some years an interest in the late sixteenth-century precursors of the novel – the great mine of the ore refined in Shakespeare's plays – I came eventually to the plays themselves. No longer the voice of authority but shrewd commentary on Elizabethan–Jacobean life, the plays gained a potential for me that earlier I had not imagined possible. They were at once images of reality and works of art; they were metaphorical transformations of life – profoundly critical, generous, passionate and rich with significance. But 'significance' is flexible in application. Elizabethan fiction taught me to look for it in concrete experience. This does not trivialise the art; on the contrary, I believe, it makes it possible for art to be serious and for Shakespeare's tragedies to have a continuing, even if not a universal, significance.

All quotations from Shakespeare's plays in the text, for convenience, are taken from Arden editions. Line references are given in parentheses following each quotation or at the end of a series of quotations.

In the writing of any work on so common a subject of discussion, there are many debts incurred. I am particularly grateful to Linden Peach for sympathetic advice in the early, uncertain stages of writing and for his constant encouragement. For their comments on drafts of various chapters I am grateful to Eleanor Margolies, Angela Matysiak and Laurene Brooks. I thank Sandra Margolies for editorial rescue work and for tolerating the obsessive behaviour that can be generated by a book nearing completion.

I wish to thank the Deutsche Shakespeare Gesellschaft whose annual Shakespeare conferences in Weimar, bringing together from many countries students of Shakespeare and performers of the plays, have provided fertile ground for new understanding. And I am grateful for their generosity in inviting me to Weimar and giving me a platform for testing my ideas.

Discussions with Andreas Kreßler of the Humboldt University of Berlin and Martin Procházka of the Czech Academy of Sciences, begun at Weimar and continued over the years, have given me fresh perspectives and helped to clarify my thinking, for which I thank them. In the

Shakespeare course for English and Drama students at Goldsmiths'
College, which we teach together, Simon Trussler, Bill Naismith and I
have for years debated our disagreements about the plays. The openness
of and commitment to these discussions have, I think, made them
valuable for all of us, and I thank Simon and Bill.

Finally, perhaps like all lecturers, I have an enormous debt to students
over the years who have argued seriously about the plays and convinced
me that Shakespeare matters. Their willingness to explore ideas and to
criticise, their good sense and good humour have been a constant but
incalculable influence on this book, for which I am grateful.

David Margolies
New Cross, London

In memory of
Jeanette Margolies and Willy Margolies, my parents,
Murray Berman and Frank Pollatsek,

and for
Lillian Berman

—*those who first taught me
to understand theory through practice*

CHAPTER I

Introduction

If Shakespeare's learning and morality now loom larger than his sense of real life, that may have something to do with the bias of literary studies. When drama becomes the subject of academic study, plays are most easily treated as literary texts, and their emphases change. Drama's attraction for the Elizabethans, as probably for people in all ages, was neither life itself, nor patterns divorced from life, but a transformation of life. However, literary studies went through a period of embarrassment about the 'life' part, bemoaning 'the unseemly rush from word to world', and that uneasiness with non-literary reality still affects the study of literature. English departments seem less happy discussing the worlds depicted in literary works than the patterns into which the material is shaped. Concern with the abstract distinguishes the professionals from non-academic readers interested in immediate life. This distinction is real (the study of literature *is* different from reading for pleasure) but too much weight is placed on it: literature and drama, for the most part, have been written for people whose concern with the life that is transformed in art is at least equal to their interest in its process of transformation.

That does not mean that Shakespeare's plays directly reflect their own historical actuality. We learn nothing about Hamlet from studying Elsinore; historical Venice offers no clues to Shylock's behaviour. In fact, the assumption of a literal relation changes the emphases in the plays. Thus, with the role of the ghost in *Hamlet* or the witches in *Macbeth*: in the literary text 'is the ghost real?' or 'are the witches actually there?' can seem important questions, whereas in the theatre we see (or at least hear) them and therefore they exist – they have a primary existence on stage.

Literalism can also be more than a crude privileging of literal meaning. When Osric brings Hamlet the challenge to a duel with Laertes, the language they speak is so rhetorically elaborate as to make it almost incomprehensible, even for the participants – 'Is't not possible to understand in another tongue?' asks Horatio (V.ii.125). This atmosphere of foppish, courtly behaviour, where elegance and novelty are much more important than the clarity of the message, is what the drama is here organised to convey – if the scholar Horatio has difficulties in grasping the meaning, no one else need feel shy about lack of comprehension. But the expectation for a literary text is that the words lead us to meaning, and especially if interpretative footnotes have been lavished on the scene, the logical-referential function of the words is elevated. The scene then appears to be a transfer of information, instead of a construction of attitude. Its content has been changed.

Drama encompasses a range of ways of making meaning that are unavailable to literature; a performance is a coming together of different modes that interact. Of these the literary is only one element of many, and literary statements are modified, qualified, complicated, even reversed in meaning through the force of other systems of expression. The study that follows is restricted to a narrower range of signifying practices than performance – it *is* literary. But I hope I have been able to maintain a sense that the subject is plays rather than static texts, plays that were designed to entertain an audience.

To look for thematic continuity in plays that I regard as entertainment may appear a mistaken attempt to combine opposites. The practices of literary study have often made enjoyment seem irreconcilable with serious thought. But what is serious and what is enjoyable may not be immediately obvious. Even which things in the plays are considered to be meaningful, and the level at which meaning is located, undergoes historical change (if meaning was once found, say, in Viola's witty protection of her 'innocence', it is more likely to be seen today in the carnival quality of Illyria; if meaning in *King Lear* was once found in the character of Cordelia, in recent years it may be relocated to her use of 'nothing' as a signifier).

In one sense Shakespeare's work has a general applicability

which has been oversold as 'universality'. He presents archetypes and patterns of being that have a relevance to most societies (dealing with such things as relations between parents and children, romantic love, honour, death), but they are anchored in historically specific experience. In a 1988 East German production of *Hamlet*, for example, it was a socialist bureaucracy that oppresses the Prince and which is confirmed as coldly authoritarian when Fortinbras takes over; in Derek Jarman's film of *The Tempest* (1980) the action takes place in a decaying mansion that suggests imperial decline. Obviously, these contexts are different from what was seen by Elizabethan and Jacobean audiences, but all productions of Shakespeare's plays, from the *Richard III* of the Rustaveli Company from Soviet Georgia or the *King Lear* of the Rock Kabuki Super Ichiza from Japan to this season's repertory of the Royal Shakespeare Company, are only specific embodiments of the general patterns and archetypes formulated by Shakespeare – they are, and are not, the same plays.

This variety is possible because the plays can be interpreted on different levels of reality. People can have different notions of the action that is taking place, or even what the play is about. Is *Hamlet* about an intellectual who cannot bring himself to practical action? about legal questions of usurpation? about the corruption of the Court? about sons revenging wronged fathers? The same text can be grasped in countless different ways but, if it is more than an abstract pattern, the action has to be comprehended by the audience as something concrete – an audience *brings* a reality to the archetype in order to make sense of it. The content of the plays is thus not something fixed; it changes. *Cymbeline*, for example, neglected for decades, has suddenly found favour and has been produced several times in recent years, with what is effectively a new content: it has metamorphosed from a string of moral tales into a play valued for its artifice, for an interweaving of narratives which is of more interest than the events themselves. Even if Shakespeare's plays (contrary to Hamlet's view) are not constructed as mirrors of their time, the significances found by audiences who attend the plays for their own pleasure are determined by their experiences of their own world. They 'find' according to what they are used to finding, and it is the motivations which function in the real world that give force and meaning to the actions and images of the play. However universal they may be, the plays are also always specific.

The play-within-the-play in *Hamlet* often serves as a convenient model of theatre practice, and Gertrude's response to it as audience is instructive. The player queen's rejection of the player king's well-intentioned suggestion of her remarriage after his death is so strenuous that, when asked by Hamlet how she likes the play, Gertrude utters the famous cliche, 'The lady doth protest too much, methinks' (III.ii.225). She makes it clear (regardless of any implications for her own character) that she judges the stage action by criteria that come from real life.

Plays as metaphors

The capacity of the plays to produce both real-life and 'universal' interpretations at the same time originates from their construction as what I would term metaphors. Metaphor comes from the Greek *metapherein*, literally, to transfer, and its fundamental property is the transferring of qualities from one thing to another. In a play this is more than a comparison of two things whose characteristics are already understood, where it may be the wit of the coupling that attracts attention; it involves the relation of the play as a whole to an outside reality. This may be as limited as a device for talking indirectly yet coherently about matters barred from discussion by tact or censorship (e.g., specific political figures), but it can also be a mode of exploration, where the significance of the behaviour that is turned into metaphor is not yet clear and the metaphor evaluates or tests it. Here the play can go beyond presenting what is already known to generate new understanding.

This functioning of metaphor is perhaps seen most clearly in contrast to analogy. Analogy is concerned with the logical relationships of the things compared. Thus, for instance, the medieval and Renaissance construction of the parallel between the human body and the body politic is directed primarily towards explaining what is the 'proper' relation of parts to whole. The equivalence drawn between head and head of state is based on *rational* perception. If, however, we look at Hamlet 'recognising' Polonius as a fishmonger (II.ii.171–219), the comparison is evaluative without being logical; it is the qualities vaguely associated with fishmonger and its figurative sense of bawd that are of primary concern. A logical relation can be constructed between Polonius's behaviour and the activity of a fishmonger but it is the associated subjective qualities, rather than the rationally perceived analogy, that here define him. The interchange achieves a clarity of attitude – it confirms Polonius as a pompous, irritating fool – but it cannot readily be rendered in a rational statement. The same functioning of language can be seen in Costard's use of 'goose' in *Love's Labour's Lost*. Without any precise meaning for the word, it is made to signal some dubious practice or verbal sleight of hand – e.g., 'O! marry me to one Frances – I smell some l'envoy, some goose in this' (III.i.118–19). It is rich in significance but not susceptible to rational restatement. Like proverbs or argument through anecdote, metaphor has a social objectivity but works by irrational means.

The plays (as entire works, not just separate scenes or passages) often function in this way as non-rational argument. This can be seen in differences in the construction of *King Lear* and *Gorboduc* (1562), one of *Lear*'s sources. The purposes of *Gorboduc* are slightly complicated because it was composed for an Inner Temple audience and Queen Elizabeth by Thomas Sackville and Thomas Norton, both Members of Parliament; the play has been seen as a warning to the Queen about the need for a clear successor to the throne. In any case, it is a rhetorically clothed illustration of the consequences of certain clearly defined actions – viz., the retirement of the king and the division of the kingdom. The subject treated explicitly by the play is what it is really interested in – not as actuality (not King Gorboduc's demise and the subsequent anarchy) but as real action that could be taken in the world of the audience. The moral arises directly from the actions, without need of much interpretation.

King Lear, on the other hand, does not *illustrate* an argument; there is no pre-formed argument to which the play is tailored or which can be seen to encompass most of the play's material. The experience presented is the primary material, i.e., it is not there as auxiliary to a moral and is not exhausted by any moral. This is not to say the play lacks argument, but it does not conform to something *external* to the play. The argument is its own, arising from the action as a total experience.

Gorboduc has its dramatic significances, short-lived though they may have been in English stage history: it was the first English tragedy and the first English blank verse drama, and it is rhetorically interesting. But it lacks fluidity. The debating-style balance and even-handedness of argumentation in the speeches suggest through the form that equilibrium has a moral value but the chief effect of the rhetoric is decorative; like the barrister's wig or wood panelling in the bank manager's office, it gives the speeches dignity and makes the words seem serious.

In contrast, *King Lear* works through an experiential perspective such as Gertrude brings to the play-within-the-play: meaning comes most powerfully through the action as if it were real-life experience. This is not to suggest that the play lacks ideas, but the ideas are tested in terms of what they mean in practice for people's lives. The play organises experience to show through action what the behaviour it embodies means.

At one level, experiential testing of ideas seems the obvious means for Shakespeare to use. As well as needing a 'story' to please an audience, Shakespeare worked during a period of rapid change. In such a time the terms of evaluation are so fluid that they cease to be adequate for making judgements of real life. Good and bad, the fixed points of evaluation, become unfixed and, as their social context shifts, their values shift as well. Falstaff, complaining about the pain in his great toe, says, 'A pox of this gout! or a gout of this pox!' (2 *Henry IV*, I.ii.244–5). In this he reverses the roles of the standard and what is measured against it. The pox as the index of badness for the gout is negated, for the gout is made the index of the badness of the pox. In denying measure that exists outside the will of the individual, Falstaff in effect makes objective judgement impossible. This is probably the most subversive line in Shakespeare's work, but the humour belies the seriousness. Community of values, shared to the extent of needing no explanation, is disintegrating. The premises change while the words remain the same; the words have become hollow or unreliable.

Perhaps the best-known instance of this is the word 'honour'. Antony's 'Friends, Romans, countrymen' speech from *Julius*

Caesar (Act III, scene 2) is unusual in that the evolving sense of meaning of the word is maintained in the cliche. 'Honourable', which first appears to refer to a vague, socially directed goodness and upright behaviour, shifts in the speech to include something like a self-interested manipulation of an image of public good from a position of authority. The cliche 'he is an honourable man' preserves this dubious quality. Honour is deconstructed and its existence as social virtue negated in Falstaff's catechism on honour towards the end of 1 *Henry IV*:

> What is honour? A word. What is in that word honour? What is that honour? Air. A trim reckoning! Who hath it? He that died a-Wednesday. Doth he feel it? No. Doth he hear it? No. 'Tis insensible, then? Yea, to the dead. But will it not live with the living? No. Why? Detraction will not suffer it. Therefore I'll none of it. Honour is a mere scutcheon – and so ends my catechism. (V.i.134–41)

In Prince John of Lancaster's treacherous behaviour to the surrendered rebels in 2 *Henry IV* (IV.i) and in the young king's manipulation of his questioning soldiers in *Henry V*, honour becomes even more problematic. And whereas the old nobility in *Richard II* – Gaunt and York – could talk about honour and be certain about what they referred to, Hamlet finds an unresolvable contradiction between the image conveyed by the word and the actuality he faces. For Shakespeare, by the time he wrote *Hamlet*, words alone could no longer evaluate experience adequately; something of the experience had to be reproduced *at the level of experience* for it to be understandable.

Contradictions such as those faced in *Hamlet* are disturbing for the audience because they destabilise what previously seemed assured, without offering any replacement certainties. The contradictions between the convention and the actuality, between old word and new meaning, do not inhere in word or convention; they are rooted in the experience presented. The conflict between Polonius's position of worthiness and his personal corruption, at the experiential level, cannot be escaped. Yet it can be missed when the pattern is abstracted from the concrete, allowing Polonius's role of 'concerned father' to be presented without any disturbance from his concrete behaviour as oppressive patriarch. Abstractions *feel* like certainties, like things really known, because they are above the contradictions of embedded reality and do not have to suffer the negotiation of doubts. Chancellors remain noble, dukes remain wise, heroic young kings leading their troops in battle remain devoted exclusively to the public good – because the definition of the action is separated from the concrete experience. But this changes meanings; complex truths arrived at through material interaction are reduced to truisms. When the concreteness that problematises the themes is avoided by abstraction, the plays become fossils.

The insistence on finding abstract content separate from a material embodiment is similar to the joke about the man who took home every evening from the factory where he worked a wheelbarrow full of straw. Each day the guard at the gate searched through the straw but could find nothing and let the man pass. Finally, when he was about to retire, the guard said to him: 'Look, I know you've been stealing something all these years, but I can't figure out what. Every night I go through the straw in your wheelbarrow but I can't find a thing. Now that you're about to retire, won't you tell me what it is you're stealing?' The man looked at the guard and said, simply, 'Wheelbarrows!' The play is not a vessel that *contains* the truth; it embodies it.

The problem of abstraction occurs not only in relation to philosophy or morality or questions of state. Treating the plays as mirrors of history can also be a form of abstraction. If readers are asked by the critic to make a rational comparison of the history presented in the play with their understanding of the actual history, and in that difference to read a commentary, then they must receive the play not as a hypothetical actuality, as experience, but as coded meanings from which they can reason out the significance. Thus in *Richard II*, which is concerned with two opposed ways of understanding (and ultimately of organising) society, the energies of the metaphor derive from the social transformations taking place in Shakespeare's own day. It can be interpreted in relation to the actual reign of the real King Richard II, but such historical specificity, rather than making it seem more real, distances it. If its metaphorical character is not acknowledged, the transferability of attitude that gives the play the possibility of significance disappears. Asking an audience to filter the action through a screen of historical understanding instead of experiencing it is asking them to regard plays as documentaries and ignore the fact that it is drama they are watching. Similarly, when Shakespeare re-writes *The Iliad* in *Troilus and Cressida*, even though a learned audience can gain something from recognising the changes, the meaning comes primarily from the nature of the action portrayed; historical reflection only *modifies* that understanding.

In the same way, an abstract structure of causation can be established whereby the play is made to depend on a single action – something like 'tragic flaw' – which, it can be argued rationally, is what produces the subsequent catastrophe. Thus, for instance, the deteriorated personal relationships in *King Lear* are sometimes attributed to the unnatural state of affairs produced by the king's abdication – the single action is given the whole play's load of significance. In the same way Macbeth's murder of Duncan or Antony's return to Egypt are invested with the causation of the disaster and a simplistic moral for the plays can then be rationally deduced. It is simplistic because it ignores the unstable context in which the momentous actions occur. Lear's world is shown by the play *not* to have been well-ordered – if it had been his abdication would have been inconvenient rather than disastrous. The tragedies show that the conditions of chaos – presented concretely in the experience in the plays – are as important as the single great tragic actions that only precipitate (rather than cause) the disaster.

The context in which Shakespeare is studied has made the abstract seem more valuable than the concrete. What happens to the value of the plays if their Grand Issues are reduced to experience? The loss of cultural status that the plays may suffer is more than compensated for by an increased potential to affect an audience. Issues such as 'Man's Place in the Universe', 'the Nature of Justice', 'Responsibility', or whatever abstraction one uses to construct the themes of the plays, are embedded in the elements of ordinary life – personal desires, needs, relationships. The choice between submission to the slings and arrows of outrageous fortune and the quietus made with a bare bodkin gains its significance from the audience's grasp of such things as the insolence of office and the law's delay in real life. The ordering of values produced by the grand pattern of the play reflects on concrete life to make greater sense of real existence. The metaphors in the grand scheme of the plays thus make greater coherence of the real-life attitudes from which they are generated.

Ostensibly, coherence is provided by the ideology available to the audience. There was only one elaborated intellectual system available to the Elizabethans – a late medieval hierarchical philosophy usually referred to as 'the Great Chain of Being'.[1] This representation of the universe pictured a hierarchical order that assured a place for everything in the world in the Great Chain of Being and gave it a rank. It was an elegant, generous philosophy, and comforting in its harmonious totality, but unfortunately it did not accord with material reality. As a guide to making sense of the real world, it was useless. It could not explain the rapid changes taking place in society or offer reassurance in regard to the widely-remarked decline in behaviour. There was shock at things horrifying and incomprehensible, from personal suffering to social conditions that seemed beyond anyone's control. The drastic inflation in the sixteenth century is well known. The standard of English diet declined. Vagabondage became an increasing problem. Yet display of luxury increased. The progress of individuals through the stages of a craft, from apprentice to journeyman to master, was increasingly difficult, and expectations of self-improvement were frustrated. It was a world that was less and less working the way it was supposed to. Greed and corruption, crime, usury, self-serving, social disregard, and the destabilising of honour by wealth became more frequently the material of popular culture. The widening gulf between rich and poor is much commented upon. Robert Greene's enormously popular Coney-Catching pamphlets (1591–2) and *A Quip for an Upstart Courtier* (1592) attacked social climbing by *nouveaux riches* and related it to oppression of the poor. The disruption of inherited order by new wealth, e.g., the selling of knighthoods by King James, is a subject of Ben Jonson's trenchant wit. In *The Alchemist*, Mammon's fantasy of what he will do when he has the philosophers' stone moves in

[1] The term 'Great Chain of Being' was popularised by E. M. W. Tillyard's *The Elizabethan World Picture*, originally published in 1943 and still current in Penguin paperback.

heroic rhetoric from sexual excess and luxury to a far-fetched gluttony:

> My foot-boy shall eat pheasants, calvered salmons,
> Knots, godwits, lampreys. I myself will have
> The beards of barbels served instead of salads;
> Oiled mushrooms; and the swelling unctuous paps
> Of a fat pregnant sow, newly cut off,
> Dressed with an exquisite and poignant sauce.

He concludes by saying:

> For which, I'll say unto my cook, 'There's gold;
> Go forth, and be a knight!'
> (II.ii.80–7)[2]

The dependence of rank on money is not worth direct comment by Mammon; it is so common that it is taken for granted.

Drama and fiction provided no sociological analysis but they dealt with the Big Questions of Life on a scale that could be grasped in terms of people's own lives.

Continuity in the tragedies

If Shakespeare's tragedies can reasonably be seen as provoking a coherent emotional response to the world in their contemporary audience, it is also reasonable to assume that we can find a continuity between them. The subject of the plays is the same contradictory, evolving society, and it is the same man who is organising experience into metaphors. That is the argument of this study. Although the literal subject changes from play to play, from *Hamlet* on there is a thematic coherence – the plays are all metaphors of social disintegration. Each succeeding tragedy, in a different playworld, shows a world at a further stage of decline.

The plays are written to entertain an audience but it is Shakespeare's complex response to the world changing around him that gives them such energy and motivation. In *Hamlet* he first confronts directly the problem of social degeneration. The outrage noticeable in the later tragedies is also present here but is

[2] Ben Johnson, *Three Comedies*, ed. M. Jamieson (1978: Penguin, Harmondsworth).

not coherent; the tragedy has structural problems. Shakespeare then entered a period of experimentation dominated by his use of forms that are consciously artificial and the construction of plays that tease the audience with conflicting expectations – the so-called Problem Plays. These three plays (*Troilus and Cressida*, *All's Well that Ends Well* and *Measure for Measure* and also a few others that have the characteristics but not the title of Problem Play) gain their effects essentially through the generation of contradictions that are unresolvable within the plays. Thus *All's Well that Ends Well* concludes with what is formally the heroine's success – she wins back her husband – but which is also a disaster in its content – he is not worth the winning. (First prize, two weeks in North Dakota; second prize, three weeks in North Dakota.) In *King Lear* Shakespeare resolves the structural problem of *Hamlet* and abandons the contrived contradiction between form and content to produce a tragedy where plot carries the meaning and the material bears an inescapable resemblance to the world of the audience. *Macbeth* continues the social understanding of *King Lear*, but moves it from a social landscape to a struggle within the individual (in the manner of classical tragedy), where the hero retains social feelings that conflict irremediably with his recognition of his own anti-social actions. *Antony and Cleopatra*, which follows next, depicts a playworld one step further in social disintegration: the world of Rome lacks the understanding Macbeth gained about the need for social integration and is unable to recognise social virtues. Heroism is no longer possible; there is no place for Antony.

Coriolanus cannot recognise that he has any social being and is effectively destroyed by his hypertrophied individualism. *Timon of Athens* also shows a world with even less integration, where the bonds between humans are almost entirely gone. But, because expressive possibilities are related to the subject of discussion, *Coriolanus* and *Timon of Athens* are relatively barren poetically; they cannot generate social resonance of expression from playworlds that deny social relations.

King Lear is the first play I discuss because it is the most obviously social and because there is most agreement about its social nature. Chapter II considers the changing Elizabethan–Jacobean world, what is tragic in *Lear* and how Shakespeare makes the issues complex. Chapter III deals with *Hamlet*. While it might seem more logical to follow chronology and discuss *Hamlet* before *Lear*, I thought it would be less contentious to consider it in the light of the arguments in regard to *Lear*. This also makes more prominent Shakespeare's difficulties with structure in *Hamlet*, highlighting the problems of definition, and thus Chapter IV examines the 'objectification' of tragedy and *King Lear*'s resolution of the problem of subjectivity in *Hamlet*. In Chapter V *Macbeth* is considered in terms of a continuation of the argument of *King Lear*, internalised in the hero. The specific content of the tragedy (the problem faced by the hero, not the story of his 'downfall') is dealt with and also how it can be understood as tragic. Chapter VI, on *Antony and Cleopatra*, looks at the continuation of the theme of *Macbeth*, specifically the impossibility of a full humanity in an inhumane society.

Coriolanus and *Timon of Athens* are examined in Chapter VII as the final steps in Shakespeare's portrayal of social disintegration. Chapter VIII summarises the progress of Shakespeare's tragic argument and takes an overview of thematic continuity.

The absence of *Othello* from the main argument may seem strange. An appendix devoted to this play argues that it is of fundamentally different character from the other tragedies. Rather than creating response from conflicts in the playworld, it maximises conflict of content and form, in the manner of the problem plays – it is a Problem Tragedy.

CHAPTER II

King Lear

King Lear offers neither the fascination of Hamlet's melancholy nor the horror of the Macbeths' actions, yet it deals with a subject that in some vague way is seen as being of deeper importance than that of other Shakespeare plays. Even if this is identified as old age or Christian learning, it is recognised that the play also offers serious comment on matters of concern to the society as a whole, such as injustice, power, the distribution of wealth. The perspective from which these questions are viewed, as well as their content, is social. Through the consequences shown in the brutal experience of the playworld, Shakespeare evaluates the new individualistic definition of Man.

Unlike the other plays where, with only a little critical wilfulness, kingship can be reduced to mystery or ceremony, Lear's reign is presented in terms of actual rule. Compare it, for example, with Richard II's personalised presentation of kingship:

> Not all the water in the rough rude sea
> Can wash the balm off from an anointed king. (III.ii.54–5)

Here the crown becomes numinous – the usurpers lifting their 'vassal hands against my head,/ And threat the glory of my precious crown' (III.iii.89–90) – and seems to possess a power independent of what it symbolises. Or compare it with Henry VI's formulaic presentation: he sits upon a molehill in 3 *Henry VI* discoursing on how the life of a simple shepherd is preferable to that of a king:

> the shepherd's homely curds,
> His cold thin drink out of his leather bottle,
> His wonted sleep under a fresh tree's shade,
> All which secure and sweetly he enjoys,

Is far beyond a prince's delicates –
His viands sparkling in a golden cup,
His body couched in a curious bed,
When Care, Mistrust, and Treason waits on him.
(3 *Henry VI*, II.v.47–54)

Or again compare it with the opportunistic understanding of the mystery of kingship that Richard III presents, as when he plays at refusing the crown: 'Alas, why would you heap this care on me?/ I am unfit for state and majesty' (III.vii.203–4). When Lear says, 'O! I have ta'en/ Too little care of this' (III.iv.32–3), the reference is focused on particular people and it reflects his awareness of the inadequacy of his rule; the perspective is social rather than personal.

The play is not just a subjective view presented through a character but a demonstration. At the risk of being somewhat mechanistic, I want to consider the model of society presented in *Lear* and then examine what Shakespeare does with it, how significance is developed through the interaction of the different types of behaviour.

The tragedy has an extraordinary scope. The number of characters playing significant parts (i.e., where they affect the action through a will of their own rather than merely as instruments of someone else) is unusually large. The number of households strains the notion of unity and an exceptional range of the spectrum of social class is included. Shakespeare's use of Poor Tom, for example, would stretch the limits of tragic decorum in giving so much weight to a personage of low rank were it not that Poor Tom is actually the disguised Edgar. Unlike the gravediggers in *Hamlet* who are laughed at (however profound the scene may really be), Poor Tom is given sufficient tragic space to require that he be taken seriously, contrary to most contemporary dramatic treatment of lower-class characters. Poor Tom's poverty is more than convention – he does not 'usurp the beggary he was never born to' like the posing Duke Vincentio of *Measure for Measure* (III.ii.90); he feigns poverty to conceal himself amidst *real* deprivation. The technique of double social status was well developed in Elizabethan popular literature (notably in Robert Greene's *Pandosto* and *Menaphon*). In combining in one role the noble Edgar's painful tending of his father with Poor Tom's absolute poverty, Shakespeare emphasises the reality of the misery endured by the Elizabethan homeless, without breaching the decorum required of the tragedian.

The 'double-plot', apart from any other aesthetic function, has the effect of multiplying characters and action, which provides, like pollsters' surveys, something that seems less simple anecdote and more 'valid sample'; it provides types that, because the play repeats them, can be seen to be types. This is apparent when the Edmund figure, for example, is compared with Shakespeare's source for the Gloucester plot, Sidney's *Arcadia* (Book II, chapter 10). Sidney makes the illegitimate Plexirtus simply an irredeemable 'bastard' whose treatment of his father Leonatus, King of Paphlagonia, is peculiar to that relationship. If it has any feeling of typicality, that is the result of the style of presentation, the use of a folk type, rather than any pseudo-rational or sociological sense of type; whereas in *King Lear* Edmund's behaviour, because it is paralleled by that of the wicked daughters, goes beyond personal animus and partakes of certain principles that are generalised in the society.

The personal relation of characters to their world that Shakespeare presents in *King Lear* falls into two basic types. While Gloucester, Kent, Edgar, Albany and Lear himself are clearly differentiated from one another in their personal characteristics, they also share a number of significant qualities: they adhere to tradition, are attentive to form and symbol and accept conventions, and they understand relationships to be personal and qualities to be inherent in the person. On the other hand, Goneril, Regan, Cornwall and, above all, Edmund are inner-directed, rational and empirical in their understanding of the world, and relationships for them are more subject to calculation of personal advantage than sentiment in regard to the person, and for them attributes are separable. Thus, in regard to the matter of kingship, Lear and his adherents regard him as a royal personage, not just a person filling the job of king, whereas Edmund and his associates take an opposite position and reject inherent status (as when Goneril tells the retired king to recognise 'what you rightly are' – I.iv.220).

The divergence of types (not of personalities but of positions in regard to the world) is most strikingly expressed in the opposition of Edmund and Gloucester in the second scene. This involves more than conventions of style; it is made clear that the conflict is one of fundamental outlook. Edmund states his allegiance to a nature whose principle is force rather than regularity and, in the most vigorous terms, announces his individuality.

Edmund's speech and its charged conclusion – 'Now, gods, stand up for bastards!' (I.ii.22) – contrasts sharply with the degenerated half-thoughts muttered by Gloucester in the next lines:

> Kent banish'd thus! And France in choler parted!
> And the King gone to-night! prescrib'd his power!
> Confin'd to exhibition! All this done
> Upon the gad! – Edmund, how now! What news? (I.ii.23–6)

The conflict is focused when Gloucester exits, after a speech blaming disasters and discords in countries, cities, palaces and families on astrological causes, the late eclipses in the sun and moon which 'portend no good to us' (I.ii.100–1): Edmund attacks his father's views, not for scientific error, but for their shifting of responsibility from the individual to the zodiac. The speech has the same energy that marked his entry into the scene, though now, juxtaposed to Gloucester's senile commonplaces, it has a rationality that is heroic in Edmund's personal relation to truth – it is a truth *for him* instead of mere acceptance of 'objective' reason, of a systematic truth lying outside the individual. Wielding reason to scour away the encrustations of custom, Edmund is endowed with the fresh vision of the age. He has the logic of a visionary and the intensity of an avenging angel.

Even the form of his speech is distinguished from that of the court where thoughts and attitudes are comfortably confined within the spoken lines. From his initial compact expression of an idea – 'Thou, Nature, art my goddess; to thy law / My services are bound' – which has a stable, near-congruence of language and thought, the energy rises to his breathless five lines expressing one image of self-assertion, lines that culminate in his resolution to act:

> Who in the lusty stealth of nature take
> More composition and fierce quality

Than doth, within a dull, stale, tired bed,
Go to th'creating a whole tribe of fops,
Got 'tween asleep and wake? Well then,
. . . (I.ii.1–2,11–15).

The excitement of this rationality conveyed through Edmund
has nothing to do with order or accuracy; it is perhaps more
understandable as discovery. Consider the scene in Marlowe's
Tamburlaine where the hero encounters the deficient King
Mycetes trying to hide his crown:

Tam. Are you the witty king of Persia?
Myc. Ay, marry, am I: have you any suit to me?
Tam. I would entreat you to speak but three wise words.
Myc. So I can when I see my time.
Tam. Is this your crown?
Myc. Ay: didst thou ever see a fairer?
Tam. You will not sell it, will ye?
Myc. Such another word, and I will have thee executed. Come, give
    it me.
Tam. No, I took it prisoner.
Myc. You lie; I gave it you.
Tam. Then 'tis mine.
Myc. No; I mean I let you keep it.
Tam. Well, I mean you shall have it again.
    Here, take it for a while: I lend it thee,
    Till I may see thee hemm'd with armed men.
    Then shalt thou see me pull it from thy head:
    Thou art no match for mighty Tamburlaine.
        Exit.
Myc. O gods, is this Tamburlaine the thief?
    I marvel much he stole it not away.
    (II.iv.23–41)[1]

Having labelled Tamburlaine 'thief', he is incapable of recognising that the epithet does not fit the magnificence and superiority of Tamburlaine's conduct. Mycetes' stupidity and weakness
are tied to his inability to understand anything except through
inherited formulations or to examine anything afresh. Tamburlaine's ability to judge a concrete reality and his knowledge that
the respect accorded inherited title has nothing to do with merit

[1] Christopher Marlowe, *The Complete Plays*, ed. J. B. Steane (1973: Penguin,
Harmondsworth).

are likewise a power (which is extended to its limits in *Doctor Faustus*). Tamburlaine overthrows traditional order, de-mystifies hereditary kingship and asserts a fierce individuality that is a forerunner of Edmund's. This is the hallmark of the revolutionary bourgeoisie, the ceaseless changing of conditions and clarity of vision that so excited Marx in the *Manifesto of the Communist Party*:

All fixed, fast-frozen relations, with their train of ancient and venerable prejudices and opinions, are swept away, all new-formed ones become antiquated before they can ossify. All that is solid melts into air, all that is holy is profaned, and man is at last compelled to face with sober senses, his real conditions of life, and his relations with his kind.[2]

Goneril and Regan share in this rationality, which is the quality most evident in their dispassionate consideration of Lear's impulsive behaviour (in the last lines of the first scene). The nearest they come to wickedness here is Goneril's calculating 'Pray you, let us hit together: if our father carry authority with such disposition as he bears, this last surrender of his will but offend us' (I.i.302–5). Though this comment reflects self-interest rather than filial concern, it is a just evaluation of the difficulty that is likely to ensue if Lear continues in the role of king. His reported conduct in scene iii bears out her judgement, but she adds a note of antagonism to her rational posture: 'Old fools are babes again, and must be us'd/ With checks as flatteries, when they are seen abus'd' (I.iii.20–1). The point is that this is not merely a clash of wills; Goneril's practical–rational sense is in opposition to Lear's ceremonial dignity. With less of the excitement of discovery, Goneril shares Edmund's sense of the world; they are the same type.

The play's exaggeration of types has the effect of sharpening the opposition between them. It is not individual stupidity as such that accounts for Lear's and Gloucester's behaviour; rather, they both believe completely in and rely on tradition and form. Goneril, Regan and Edmund, on the other hand, are united in intense pursuit of their own desires through rational assessment of circumstances. But Shakespeare does not offer judgement

[2] In K. Marx and F. Engels, *Collected Works*, Vol. 6 (1976: Lawrence and Wishart, London), p. 487.

according to type. Even in their first introduction the representatives of stable order are at the very least irritating, while
Edmund's individualism is certainly attractive as well as shocking.
And even though Edmund's plotting must almost by definition
be seen as wicked, Goneril and Regan's behaviour, until the end
of Act II, is harsh rather than wicked. Judgement comes not from
identification of the type, the Western's good guys in white hats,
bad guys in black, but from the *consequences* of attitudes, what
they lead to in practice. The point is not a clear moral like 'don't
divide the kingdom' of *Gorboduc* (one of the play's major sources)
– this division has already been decided before the play com-
mences and the distribution is dramatically completed in the first
scene; rather it is what certain attitudes and positions in regard to
the world mean when tested in practice. That is, the actions of the
play are a dramatic testing of real social attitudes.

This testing in practice is not so much a matter of the
development of his skill in characterisation as a recognition of the
contradictory forces operating on individuals (individual psychology in the major tragedies, even *Macbeth*, is secondary to
organisation of social values). After *Richard III*, where good and
bad are still mechanically opposed, the qualities of characters are
given less distinct separation and embody more of the contradictions that emerge from life in a complex, rapidly changing
society. In *Henry IV* (both parts), for example, the prince's
personal qualities are not neatly divisible into good and bad (as
are, say, Richard II's) but are a mixture that reflects the influence
of both the socially approved Lord Chief Justice and the disreputable Falstaff. This makes them more representative of actual
social conditions (i.e., more typical) and also more credible in
naturalistic terms.

Even in the beginning of *King Lear*, where opposition is
clearly signalled, there is no direct emergence of good and bad.
From the first scene of the play the tradition-directed and
inner-directed types are brought into dramatic, formal opposition. Lear is making *formal* distribution of his kingdom (the
divisions have already been decided upon, as the opening six lines
and the existence of a previously prepared map indicate). He
demands first from each of his daughters a reassurance of their
love for him, a formalising of relationship which they would have

expected and been prepared for, and to which, with the exception of Cordelia, they glibly respond. The sweeping rhetorical flow of Lear's ceremonial love test is interrupted by Cordelia's first aside, and thereafter the abstract language is in conflict with concrete directness. Lear, Goneril and Regan use a stilted diction appropriate to public ceremony:

> Dearer than eye-sight, space and liberty;
> . . .
> A love that makes breath poor and speech unable;

and

> With shadowy forests and with champains rich'd,
> With plenteous rivers and wide-skirted meads,
>   (I.i.55, 59, 63–4).

The lines are mostly end-stopped, making the speeches sound consciously rhetorical, in an old-fashioned, *Gorboduc*-like declamatory way. Cordelia's lines, on the other hand, are usually run-on (I quote single lines in isolation because that shows it strikingly):

> You have begot me, bred me, lov'd me: I
> . . .
> Why have my sisters husbands, if they say
> . . .
> That lord whose hand must take my plight shall carry
>   (I.i.95, 98, 100)

This (with the intervening lines, of course) is more like conversational speech and is in keeping with Cordelia's greater concern for substance than form. However, language differences in no way make clear the opposition and the 'sides' cannot be distinguished by their linguistic habits. Kent, for instance, shares Lear's formal and regular lines; Regan and Goneril partake of a formality that may disguise their individualised approach, and their interchange that closes the scene is as direct and concrete as Cordelia's speech (LL.282–307).

It is development in the action that clarifies the types and their significance. Unlike *Hamlet*, where events can be seen in the hero's perspective, in *King Lear* the types are made dramatically objective. Their significance emerges from their interaction with others and consequences in practice. Qualities may initially appear to be different from what eventually emerges in the action (e.g., the freedom Edmund appears to possess at first becomes more akin to alienation by the end). Characteristics are not uniform, single qualities; their meaning is realised not in isolation but in the way they function in a context.

Rationality

The rationality that distinguishes the modern, individually motivated characters initially seems a characteristic that is potentially very positive. Since it is also one of the main 'virtues' on which our industrial system and the educational system that serves it are based, an audience of today may regard it as natural and be less immediately disposed to question it than would an Elizabethan audience. This means we must be attentive to the way Shakespeare examines it through action rather than accepting it as merely neutral or positive.

Rationality enables Goneril and Regan to separate public behaviour from personal feelings (as they do in the first scene, in the ceremony of Lear's retirement), and Edmund, likewise, can disguise his thoughts (as we see in the second scene, where he misleads both his father and brother). Both Lear and Gloucester, on the other hand, rely on the surface of things, take things for what they appear to be. Thus in reading Edmund's letter Gloucester is immediately credulous and superficial; he not only believes it to be written by Edgar, but he also takes the content literally, never allowing the possibility of words meaning different things in different contexts. For Lear and Gloucester the word represents reality, the relations between them are fixed, and reality can then be understood directly from the word (or misunderstood, as in Lear's thinking ceremonial language conveys the actuality). A personal questioning reason is thus unnecessary because meaning, once something is uttered, is self-evident. This position is given an ironic twist by Sidney in sonnet 3 of *Astrophel and Stella*, where to describe the beauty of Stella he need only read it in her face:

> . . . in *Stella's* face I reed
> What Love and Beautie be; then all my deed
> But Copying is what in her Nature writes.[3]

---

[3] In *Elizabethan Sonnets*, ed. M. Evans (1977: Dent, London), p. 3.

The individualists, on the other hand, need reason to interpret their world. Thus when Goneril finds Lear and his followers a nuisance, in the third and fourth scenes of Act I, her tone is rational, however threatening:

> Sir,
> I had thought, by making this well known unto you,
> To have found a safe redress; but now grow fearful,
> By what yourself too late have spoke and done,
> That you protect this course, and put it on
> By your allowance; which if you should, the fault
> Would not 'scape censure, nor the redresses sleep,
> Which, in the tender of a wholesome weal,
> Might in their working do you that offence,
> Which else were shame, that then necessity
> Will call discreet proceeding. (I.iv.201–11)

Lear, in contrast, lacks both coherence and self-control. Regan and Cornwall, in deciding to put Kent in the stocks for his undisciplined behaviour before Gloucester's castle, are unpleasant but rational. Whereas Cornwall reasonably inquires why Kent calls Oswald knave, Kent himself answers only 'His countenance likes me not' (II.ii.87), in effect insisting that Oswald's failings are so obvious as to make explanation redundant.

The rationality, which in some instances may appear simply as 'reasonableness', becomes fairly quickly an 'iron logic'. In the Dutch auction of Lear's hundred knights in Act II, scene iv, Regan and Goneril play a duet of rationality that reduces the entourage from one hundred to none. Lear, with each cut, turns from one to the other – having left Goneril when she would reduce his followers to fifty, he says he will move to Regan with his hundred, to which she replies she will accept only twenty-five, making Goneril then the better prospect. Goneril then asks:

> Hear me, my Lord.
> What need you five-and-twenty, ten, or five,
> To follow in a house where twice so many
> Have a command to tend you? (II.iv.258–61)

The question is a rational one, the logic so familiar that it obscures the premises – until Lear takes them up.

Rationality itself is not altered, of course, during the play, but the attitudes associated with it change its character; it has its good as well as bad sides. Edmund's critical intelligence in regard to astrology reveals a willingness to face the world with a more accurate understanding, as when he replies to Edgar's challenge in Act V, scene iii. Edgar appears not only disguised but in chivalric disguise, following an obsolescent code, clothed in the rhetoric of chivalric tradition, and uttering his speech in old-fashioned end-stopped lines; whereas Edmund, the new man, in more conversational speech, dispenses with such formality and meets his challenger stripped of the garb of custom:

> In wisdom I should ask thy name;
> But since thy outside looks so fair and war-like,
> And that thy tongue some say of breeding breathes,
> What safe and nicely I might well delay
> By rule of knighthood, I disdain and spurn;
> Back do I toss these treasons to thy head,
> With the hell-hated lie o'erwhelm thy heart,
> Which, for they yet glance by and scarcely bruise,
> This sword of mine shall give them instant way,
> Where they shall rest for ever. Trumpets, speak.
> (V.iii.140–9)

Edmund faces Edgar in heroic individualism.

Gloucester lacks the rigour and rationality of individualism which would prevent him from relaxing into the security of ready-made opinions, generalisations worn into comfortable shape by other people's use. His sloppy self-acceptance is displayed not only in his set piece on astrology, but more importantly, in the opening interchanges of the play, where, pleased with himself for his past escapades and the jovial, socially accepted violations of propriety they suggest, he talks about Edmund's mother with an insensitivity that is at once brutal and well-meaning, befriending his son by saying how good in bed his mother was. He sees himself as pure victim in his downfall – 'as flies to wanton boys' – and disclaims personal responsibility, the very standpoint that Edmund demolishes in his attack on astrology. Lear, on the other hand, does eventually recognise his own responsibility – in the storm on the heath he says, 'I have ta'en too little care of this' – which gives him a stature much greater than Gloucester's. The ambiguous nature of rationality can be seen also in Cordelia's refusal to accommodate herself to Lear's ceremony – 'pride, which she calls plainness' (I.i.128), an extremely disruptive virtue.

Criteria of rationality

The criterion in the play that distinguishes between the good and bad uses of reason is whether or not it is *social*. Rationality can easily become rationalising, as we see in both Goneril and Gloucester. The social criterion depends on whether personal desire provides the only limits within which reason operates or whether there are 'objective' standards, social conventions acknowledged by the individual that limit the free play of reason.

The difference between the social standard and individualistic reason can be seen clearly when Cornwall is putting out Gloucester's eyes. Cornwall says although he cannot execute Gloucester without legal proceedings, 'yet our power/ Shall do a court'sy to our wrath' (III.vii.25–6) – i.e., his will is the determinant here, not really controlled by law. Kent's behaviour before the same Cornwall that got him put in the stocks – his attack on Oswald and rudeness to the Duke – is similar in its lack of control, in the wrath being the determinant to which the behaviour pays homage (Cornwall's 'know you no reverence?' is answered with 'Yes, sir; but anger hath a privilege' – II.ii.66–7), but it functions to further a socialised attitude. In contrast to this, when Cornwall moves to put out Gloucester's other eye a servant tries to make him face the limits of behaviour:

> Hold your hand, my Lord.
> I have serv'd you ever since I was a child,
> But better service have I never done you
> Than now to bid you hold. (III.vii.70–3)

The servant's social view is confirmed by Albany when he hears the news of Cornwall's death, 'Slain by his servant, going to put out/ The other eye of Gloucester':

This shows you are above,
You justicers, that these our nether crimes
So speedily can venge! (IV.ii.71–2,78–80)

Another way of stating the distinction between the different
kinds of reasoning is an extension of the criterion of socialisation,
the valuation of personal relationships. Edmund, Goneril and
Regan take an instrumental view of personal relations. Thus in
the interchange between Edmund and Edgar that follows
Gloucester's reading the forged letter, Edgar believes his brother
on the basis of a relationship between brothers, whereas Edmund
has nothing of the affective attitude that is part of the relationship
and merely uses it to further an end external to it. Similarly,
Goneril and Regan, in Lear's love test of the first scene, can
alienate the relationship with their father and describe it in a
rhetoric that bears no relation to what it really is. This is
contrasted to Cordelia, who insists on talking in terms of what is
actually a personal relationship, the 'bond' of a relationship
experienced in real life. Her use of 'bond' is to signify a way of life
in which the real relationship at once is taken for granted and also
breeds affection; it is carried on as a matter of course rather than
as a special performance – it may even be entered into without
choice (as with parent and child) – but it relates two people
materially and particularly to each other (a specific child to a
specific parent) and makes them mutually dependent. Goneril's
and Regan's words evoke no sense of mutuality and would be
more in keeping with 'bond' as a contractual arrangement,
transferable and not personal. This is how it is understood in *The
Merchant of Venice*, which is one reason why Shylock's insistence
on the particularity of Antonio's bond to him (he will accept no
equivalent value) so disturbs the others. Lear's understanding,
superficially in accord with that of his elder daughters, must be
influenced by this sense, in which case Cordelia's loving to a
degree commensurate with her bond would indicate to him, not
depth of feeling but obligation without willingness.

Edmund was able to dissociate himself from the blinding of his
father when Cornwall advised him to accompany the departing
Goneril and said 'the revenges we are bound to take upon your
traitorous father are not fit for your beholding' (III.vii.7–9) –

i.e., Edmund slips out of the relationship for the moment – and Regan constructs Gloucester in instrumental terms, terms only of what is in accord with her particular interests, calling him 'ingrateful fox' and 'filthy traitor'. Gloucester is not party to Regan's cause – he has not been entrusted by her with anything – and therefore he cannot betray it; rather, in terms of the relations between the characters that are presented to us on stage, Regan and Cornwall take hospitality from Gloucester and it is they, not he, who should be grateful. He alludes to this in saying 'What means your Graces? Good my friends, consider/ You are my guests: do me no foul play, friends' (III.vii.30–1). Gloucester sees a material relationship; his tormentors see only an obstacle to the fulfilment of their wills.

Most telling is Shakespeare's inclusion of a character and an interchange that seem to have no purpose other than to contrast types of relationship – the Old Man in Act IV, scene i. Thrown out of his castle to 'smell his way to Dover' and tended by the second and third servants who offer a choric, social view of what has just passed, Gloucester appears and interrupts Edgar's stoical reflections on the good that inheres in bad. Attention can be focused here either on Gloucester's reflections that parallel Edgar's: 'Full oft 'tis seen,/ Our means secure us, and our mere defects/ Prove our commodities' (IV.i.19–21), for which the presence of the Old Man is in no way necessary; or attention can be directed to what the Old Man's words imply, that he helps Gloucester because they have a relationship, which makes Gloucester's need the peasant's responsibility:

> O my good Lord!
> I have been your tenant, and your father's tenant,
> These fourscore years.
> *Glou.* Away, get thee away; good friend, be gone:
> Thy comforts can do me no good at all;
> Thee they may hurt.
> *Old Man.* You cannot see your way.

When the Old Man responds to Gloucester's point about danger by saying, in effect, that Gloucester is now disabled, there is no grammatical, logical connection here; his assumption that one helps others in trouble is so basic that it need not be spoken.

Gloucester asks only for some clothing for Poor Tom, 'for ancient love', to which the peasant answers, 'I'll bring him the best 'parel that I have,/ Come on't what will' (IV.i.12–17,43,49–50). The point here is not that the peasant is an old friend of Gloucester's but that the relationship between the two men, formally that of landlord and tenant, is more than just a contractual relation; it is a relationship between people, and as such it has its affective side. Because the two men have a material connection, a shared history, they have a feeling for each other – they are parts of each other. This is the same thing as the 'bond' Cordelia described in the first scene. The first principle of their behaviour is that they are part of a shared humanity, a sharing that is felt in some measure to define who and what they are. And characteristically, the Old Man being by definition elderly, he is a representative of the older world, the world of concrete relationships now being replaced by the rationalised, contractual understanding of such as Goneril and Regan.

It is possible to chart the landscape of social types, to schematise the different social attitudes to help clarify the structure of the play (but this abstraction cannot be a substitute for the complexity of embodied relationships). The characters of *King Lear* can be placed along two axes – the axis of individuation and the axis of socialisation. Thus, in terms of individuation, Edmund is completely individualised, while Gloucester is completely conventional in his attitudes. Lear is also (at least for most of the play) conventional, but Cordelia is determinedly individual. Edgar is conventional, his father's philosophical son, as are Kent and Albany; Goneril and Regan are of course individualistic.

On the axis of socialisation, Cordelia is outstandingly social, pursuing ends that are part of the collective good. Edmund, however, pursues ends that are for his personal benefit, without regard to their social consequences or effect on others. Edgar devotes himself to public good, while (for most of the play) Lear follows his own desires. Gloucester's behaviour, although at points he shows courageous generosity, tends more to being self-satisfying than socially responsible. Kent is socially directed, as is Albany in the little we see of him, in opposition to the self-centred behaviour of Goneril, Regan and Oswald.

Such graphing of course does not reveal anything new, but it throws into relief the parallels and oppositions of characters and suggests that these are more a matter of social understanding on the part of Shakespeare than the development of the art of characterisation. The ultimate sorting of the good people and the bad is a question of socialisation – Edgar, Kent, eventually Lear, ultimately Gloucester, Cordelia, the Fool, Albany are recognised as among the good; Edmund, Goneril, Regan, Oswald, as bad. But on the individuation axis we have a different grouping – Cordelia and Edmund are together as highly individual, while Lear, Gloucester, Kent, and Edgar are conventional. We are offered four different types of behaviour: the selfish conventional (Lear), the altruistic conventional (Edgar), the selfish individual or individualistic (Edmund) and the socially individualised or altruistic individual (Cordelia). The virtue of Cordelia, which is undisputed, is then seen to be not simply the following of social good but an active, critical relation to reality which could be mistaken for pride. She has the virtue of humility, according to the precept in Benjamin Franklin's *Autobiography*: 'Imitate Jesus and Socrates' (1964: Yale University Press, New Haven, p. 150). Cordelia, seeking to change the world in which she moves, is thus superior to the equally selfless Edgar because his adherence to convention, courageous though it may be, involves an acceptance of the structure of the world that produced such tragedy. His commitment to righting wrongs does not extend to the *causes* of those wrongs. Cordelia's relation to reality, although it must necessarily produce a greater range of conflicts, is more strenuous and more rigorous. Her actions are directed towards a social good, validated not in abstraction but in experience.

The disintegration of Lear's consciousness

A sociology of *King Lear*, however much it is elaborated, does not go beyond the representation of social forces in the play; it is necessary to explain how the story of a self-centred, irascible and irritating old man can evoke a greater emotional response from audiences than any other Shakespeare play. Why should anyone care?

The emotional effect of the play is caused not by the witnessing of so much pain or recognition of its social accuracy –

these are only the raw materials – but by the integration of the objective dramatic events with the subjective perception of the audience. The latter alone gives judgement but not the basis for it, while the former provides information for a social policy, perhaps, but not the motive. In *Lear* the feeling of events is brought out by their being reflected in a not particularly perceptive consciousness: the audience, following Lear, is made to focus on each aspect in turn. Outrage, rather than sympathy or pity, is the emotional driving force of the play. This outrage arises not from the presentation of physical pain or Lear's loss of children, status and well-being, but from the destruction of his vision of himself and violation of the audience's sense of what constitutes humanity. The play's matter is thus at once the most fundamentally individual and most general human experience.

The destruction of Lear's vision begins with Cordelia's interruption of the ceremony in the first scene and concludes with the shattering confrontation at the end of Act II (followed by the madness on the heath). When Cordelia fails to fulfil Lear's expectations, insisting on playing the love test in terms of her real feelings, not the ceremonial responses given by her sisters, Lear is outraged. This outrage finds a seemingly appropriate application in the external world: he banishes Cordelia, re-establishing his sense of control over the external world and further confirming it by banishing Kent who attempts to hinder him. Lear is obviously unsettled by these events but, however painful they may be, the injury is personal; i.e., the hurt does not demand a new understanding of the world and is containable within his old thinking.

In Lear's next confrontation, with Goneril, it is not just his equilibrium that is affected; he finds some problem with his understanding. In Act I, scene v, his mind moves about disjointedly, which can be a sign of the emotional impact of the rejection of a second daughter, but he also worries about being mad, voiced in response to the Fool's saying 'Thou should'st not have been old till thou hadst been wise' (I.v.41–2). When in the preceding scene he beats his head, attacking it as 'this gate, that let thy folly in,/ And thy dear judgment out' (I.iv.269–70), it is the application of his understanding that troubles him, not the possibility that he *mis*understands. The result of his actions has been poor; he must have done something wrong – but he does not question the *principles* on which he acts.

The Fool serves to emphasise the gap between understanding of the pieces and of the whole. He maintains a common sense approach to the world, cutting through the cant, correcting Lear's perception of what is before him, without however adding any new analysis. He utters proverbially and epigrammatically a content that is perceived within the same frame of consciousness as Lear's. Even if the more material expression facilitates an emotional response (from Lear and from the audience), it is often a simplistic understanding. Functioning like a chorus, the Fool gives an emphasis to and makes clearer the immediate situation, yet without making it more comprehensible. He adds the truth of 'they say' which, always lagging behind the present conceptually, cannot produce solutions. When Lear gains vision, after the heath, he no longer needs the Fool, and his own critique when he meets the blinded Gloucester in Act IV, scene vi, takes on many of the characteristics of the Fool's speech – e.g., 'No eyes in your head, nor no money in your purse? Your eyes are in a heavy case, your purse in a light: yet you see how this world goes' (IV.vi.143–6). But once he is able to grasp the material world before him, Lear goes beyond the sayings of the Fool, to generalise from specific elements of reality a penetrating social critique, as in his discourse on justice and authority (IV.vi.149–70).

When he is about to depart from Goneril's castle, his confidence in the *system* is still unshaken, which is shown by his cursing Goneril. He addresses the supernatural powers and asks them to revenge his wrong: 'Hear, Nature, hear! dear Goddess, hear!' The content of the curse, that she be deprived of gratitude, assumes that this gratitude is inseparable from raising children, is 'natural' to the parent–child relationship:

And from her derogate body never spring
A babe to honour her! If she must teem,
Create her child of spleen, that it may live
And be a thwart disnatur'd torment to her! (I.iv.273;278–81)

Lear continues to believe in an ordered nature. He does not think that changed material conditions will affect that order. He thinks his view of the world is natural, that it is not dependent on particular circumstances. Goneril's sin, then, is a sin of omission; it is a particular act that violates the social code – she has failed to do what is 'naturally' expected of her, and in cursing her, Lear calls on that 'natural' world to take its revenge on one who refuses to follow its prescribed patterns.

'Yet have I left a daughter' (I.iv.252), Lear says, and removes from Goneril's to Regan's but is diverted to Gloucester's castle, entering only after three intervening scenes.

In these scenes the character of the world in which Lear really moves (rather than thinks he moves) is developed further. As well as advancement of the Gloucester–Edmund–Edgar plot, the opposed social postures are characterised through the quarrelling of Kent and Oswald. Kent attacks Oswald's self-importance and lack of principle, calling him 'glass-gazing' and 'a bawd in way of good service' (II.ii.16,18) and accuses him of being made by a tailor (II.ii.52–3) – i.e., the clothing, rather than honest merit, gives him his rank. Kent takes a position of being possessed of an obvious truth: Oswald who wears the symbol of dignity, a sword, 'wears no honesty' (II.ii.70). Oswald's selfish disregard for social order is so apparent as to require no further explanation from Kent to the assembled company, and Oswald's subjective characterisation of his encounter with Kent – reversing what actually happened – gives substance to Kent's view. Most importantly, these three scenes between Lear's daughters develop the character of the individualists. This includes the subtle transformation of the material that is the subject of 'rationality', as when Goneril's rational perception that Lear's hundred knights constitute a problem evolves, in Regan's characterisation of the situation, into his 'riotous knights' who have encouraged Edgar's supposed plot against Gloucester 'To have th'expense and waste of his revenues' (II.i.93,99). She defines Lear's entourage in such a way that it includes negative values as part of the definition, the tarring with a headline approach of the tabloids that is very difficult to overcome. She begs the question – the 'facts' of the reality are filtered through her attitudes, which allows logic to arrive at only one kind of conclusion.

The point here is not so much to show the nature of the opposition Lear is up against, but to show the changed order of the world, and that this is recognised as change. Thus, when Kent refuses to control his anger and Cornwall decides to put him in the stocks, Kent matter-of-factly points out to Cornwall the significance of such an act:

Call not your stocks for me; I serve the King,
On whose employment I was sent to you;
You shall do small respect, show too bold malice
Against the grace and person of my master,
Stocking his messenger. (II.ii.125–9)

This is not pleading diplomatic immunity but making clear the relation – it is a feudal notion of representation that understands the representative as *part* of the principal for whom he carries the message. Its importance is underlined by Shakespeare's elaboration of the scene, and Gloucester, in choric fashion, stresses the enormity of stocking Kent:

Let me beseech your Grace not to do so.
His fault is much, and the good King his master
Will check him for't: your purpos'd low correction
Is such as basest and contemned'st wretches
For pilf'rings and most common trespasses
Are punish'd with: the King must take it ill,
That he, so slightly valued in his messenger,
Should have him thus restrained. (II.ii.136–43)

Ceremony, dignity, social form dissolve before this rationalised individualism. The king is no different from other nobles in the view presented by Regan. She equates the affront to the king with what would be an affront to Goneril if she were *not* to stock Kent:

My sister may receive it much more worse
To have her gentleman abus'd, assaulted,
For following her affairs. Put in his legs. (II.ii.144–6)

This all serves to emphasise the importance of Cornwall and Regan's action and prepares us for the response of Lear when he arrives in scene iv.

Lear's initial response to Kent's being in the stocks is that it is a mistake, and as such – as an error of practice – he can accommodate it in his world view: 'What's he that hath so much thy place mistook/ To set thee here?' (II.ii.11–12) His response can be seen as the opposite of Othello's Iago-induced paranoia, which concludes total disaster from small pieces of reality: Lear avoids confronting disaster by finding an interpretation that leaves his system intact. He refuses to accept that Cornwall and Regan have actually done the deed, committed the insult, that stares him in the face. His interchange with Kent is of childlike simplicity – denial, affirmation, emphatic denial, emphatic affirmation. Then follows what can be seen as a reasoned denial from Lear, that the act does not fit in with the scheme of the world as he understands it and therefore it did not happen: 'No, no; they would not.' Kent counters with the actuality – 'Yes, yes, they have.' After another two-line interchange that, with swearing, suggests Lear senses a whole system at stake here, he articulates further the grounds of his disbelief:

> They durst not do't,
> They could not, would not do't; 'tis worse than murther,
> To do upon respect such violent outrage.
> Resolve me, with all modest haste, which way
> Thou might'st deserve, or they impose, this usage,
> Coming from us. (II.iv.18,19,21–6)

Lear's most forceful objection here is that they *could* not do it. Such a deed is impossible within the very limits of civilisation as Lear knows it; it is humanly impossible. But such impossibility is a matter of rules, not feasibility. If you respond to an ungrammatical utterance of mine by saying, 'You can't say that', I can legitimately reply, 'I just have'. That may terminate the conversation but it does not make the participants disappear. Lear's society, the *organisation* of people, has disintegrated but its members, now isolated units, remain, uncontrolled and uninhibited by former conventions. Even if he does not recognise it himself, Lear's retinue, now very much diminished, certainly has. As the Fool proverbially expresses it: 'Let go thy hold when a great wheel runs down a hill, lest it break thy neck with following' (II.iv.69–71). The attitudes seen in stocking Kent are no longer an exceptional violation of social codes but now are the guide to conduct.

What the event means for Lear personally is demonstrated when, still unwilling to accept that this outrage was consciously done, he goes to seek Regan. He is violently disturbed when reality is unmoved by his will and is reduced to short bursts of rage instead of coherent statements. His frustration is seen in his repetition of Gloucester's language, as if the absurdity of the imperative without corresponding action is obvious – 'Inform'd them! Dost thou understand me, man?' (II.iv.96). Yet he tempers his rage, recognising the possibility that Cornwall and Regan may in fact, as they claim, be disabled by illness. But when Lear looks again at Kent in the stocks it confirms for him that he is being resisted consciously and wilfully, and that the social reality is no longer controllable by him. The disagreement is well beyond philosophic differences; it is charged with energy, with rage, with frustration, with hostility that come from a struggle for survival, material advantage and status. This is now a point of real confrontation, not just a conflict between different images of the world.

The character of the confrontation changes for Lear when Regan takes Goneril's side, giving them a single position in opposition to Lear. Lear has tried to separate Regan's behaviour from Goneril's, still on the basis of whether or not they adhere to his system. He says to Regan:

> thou better know'st
> The offices of nature, bond of childhood,
> Effects of courtesy, dues of gratitude;
> Thy half o'th'kingdom hast thou not forgot,
> Wherein I thee endow'd. (II.iv.175–9)

Goneril's misbehaviour, and the misbehaviour that Regan's conduct constantly verges upon, have been regarded by Lear as failure to perform that which they should, as sins of omission. But the unity of the two sisters in denying Lear has a power greater than simply doubling the debt to natural behaviour – it begins to suggest *positively* a new conduct against which the old sanctions cannot be effectively invoked. Lear, having lost command, no longer curses but mocks:

> I do not bid the thunder-bearer shoot,
> Nor tell tales of thee to high-judging Jove.
> Mend when thou canst; be better at thy leisure.
> (II.iv.225–7)

Lear accepts he has lost, that his daughters have cheated, broken
the rules, but his capacity to mock suggests that he still feels the
rules to be there, to be operable if not compelling.

Lear is at last completely disabused when Goneril and Regan
progressively reduce the number of knights he will be allowed in
his entourage to the point where Goneril says:

> What need you five-and-twenty, ten, or five,
> To follow in a house where twice so many
> Have a command to tend you?' (II.iv.259–61).

With the focus on the word 'need', the two systems are at last
brought into immediate, direct confrontation. Lear is forced to
see that it is not simply that his daughters are failing to do what
he expects of them (i.e., still employing his world-view but not
practising it), but that they are following a different scheme of
their own, that their world is organised in a different way. The
cold rationality they employ is similar to the power of abstracted
reason exercised by Shylock in *The Merchant of Venice* when
Portia, appearing as the learned justice Balthazar, says, 'Then
must the Jew be merciful': 'On what compulsion must I?'
(IV.i.178–9). Mercy is not written into the contract. Lear then
argues – is forced to articulate – the basic values of his system
without just assuming them or framing his argument entirely
within the system, as he had done hitherto:

> O! reason not the need; our basest beggars
> Are in the poorest thing superfluous:
> Allow not nature more than nature needs,
> Man's life is cheap as beast's. Thou art a lady;
> If only to go warm were gorgeous,
> Why, nature needs not what thou gorgeous wear'st,
> Which scarcely keeps thee warm. But, for true need, –
> (II.iv.262–8)

The assertion of a minimal dignity as a human, apart from mere
biological survival, which Lear had assumed without question or
even consciousness, is powerless against a system of rationalised
calculation of need. Goneril and Regan certainly recognise
human dignity – they seek it for themselves – but they do not
see it as necessary; one can be human without it. What is being
defined here is not 'need' but 'Man'. Human for Goneril and

Regan is the 'poor, bare, forked animal' Lear speaks of on the heath (III.iv.105–6) – individuals whose 'improved' qualities are individual rather than social attributes. Whereas Lear's 'human' is essentially social, existing only through social relations, Goneril and Regan's is atomistic; for them the parts do not require the whole. They are what they are even in isolation and see their humanness generated from the biology of the individual rather than from interaction with others.

Lear here at last recognises that Goneril and Regan are not offending within his system but are introducing a new system, a rationality of atomistic humanity against which his unexamined geniality of traditional relationships cannot stand. He has lost the game – not too bad in itself; and Goneril and Regan have cheated – also bearable; but they have, most importantly, changed the rules of the game, without telling Lear, and he expresses a sense of monstrous injustice, all the more monstrous because it has deprived him of the power to do anything about it.

He cannot curse, threaten in a way that assumes a system that will take revenge on those who violate it, but can merely *express* his pain and sense of disintegration:

> I will do such things,
> What they are, yet I know not, but they shall be
> The terrors of the earth. (II.iv.278–80)

The two systems here are not presented through analysis or the perspective of a character: they are made to confront each other objectively. The action reveals what the theories really mean. But the process is given significance by being presented also through Lear's eyes. Although he does not explain anything, his failure to understand is made evident and then his gradual realisation of what the new system means makes it important for the audience. Lear began in the play as someone with a consciousness restricted to a simple view of the world, seemingly incapable of comprehending any attitude not consistent with his own sense of reality. At this point he has learned that there are other *systems*, that the villains are not merely those who fail to be good but may be actively pursuing their own purposes in a totally different view of the world. Like the prisoner in Kafka's 'In the Penal Colony', who learns what his crime is in the course of a monstrous

machine's tattooing the word on his back, which is at the same
time the process of his execution, so Lear has a sudden access of
knowledge produced by his pain. But unlike Kafka's prisoner,
whose crime remains personal and whose discovery is *personal*
understanding (we never know specifically what the crime is),
Lear understands *for the audience*. His defeat coincides with his
growth in understanding, and the emotional energy of his
downfall illuminates his grasp of the limits of humanity. The
progress of his consciousness reveals for us both what different
social modes are and, in his impotent rage, their significance.

Lear's lack of reflection on his world, his blindness and almost
reflex behaviour, is brought to an end by encountering an
unassimilable obstacle – the new individualism. For the first time
Lear is able to see, the rose-tinted spectacles of convention having
been shattered by Goneril and Regan. This 'sight' is not of course
the clarity of a rational view, but an imaginative response
consistent with his earlier ceremonial approach. Even so, on the
heath he recognises his own failure – the society over which he
ruled could not meet the basic needs of all its members:

> Poor naked wretches, whereso'er you are,
> That bide the pelting of this pitiless storm,
> How shall your houseless heads and unfed sides,
> Your loop'd and window'd raggedness, defend you
> From seasons such as these? O! I have ta'en
> Too little care of this. Take physic, Pomp;
> Expose thyself to feel what wretches feel,
> That thou mayst shake the superflux to them,
> And show the Heavens more just. (III.iv.28–36)

For an audience familiar with increasing vagabondage, aware of
the ravages of enclosure, confronted by a society unable to ensure
survival, let alone dignity, for vast numbers of its members, this
must have been a profound attribution of responsibility.

Lear's recovery – or gaining – of vision, as with his growing
crisis of consciousness (his inability to assimilate in his system the
behaviour of his daughters), is a gradual process. He first
expresses concern for justice when he reflects on the mistreatment
he endures, which offends against all standards of human society
and is unjust. 'I am a man/ More sinn'd against than sinning'

(III.ii.59–60) is less a recognition of an identity with sinners than a complaint that he is himself a victim. But the theme of justice is continued in his first 'seeing', his prayer to the poor. He at least *sees* the woeful plight of the poor and accepts some share of the responsibility. The material world is no longer just a mirror of himself; he now sees it for what it is, in its horror and misery and, to some extent, in its implications.

Yet, despite the concreteness of the image in 'loop'd and window'd raggedness', Lear's description has still a generality about it – 'Poor naked wretches, *whereso'er you are*' – a selected picture rather than a direct confrontation with the material world of individual naked wretches. That of course changes when he enters the hovel to encounter Poor Tom. Poor Tom is a self-created exemplar of poverty – he is disguised – but no one is able to distinguish his condition from genuine poverty and, therefore, he is typical, a representative of the plight of the wretched poor. The degradation, the destruction of humanity, as well as the pain, is brought home completely to Lear: 'Is man no more than this?' he asks (III.iv.100–1), only a two-legged beast, subjected like other creatures to all the elements and to dumb pain? Lear witnesses in the hovel not an isolated or individual experience but a social phenomenon; he sees.

The social character of this interchange is made particularly striking in Grigori Kozintsev's film of the play (USSR, 1970). The camera gradually reveals that the hovel contains, not the one mad beggar the text allows to speak, but dozens of wretches sheltering from the storm. Similarly, the opening sequence of the film is a view of hundreds of feet, all wrapped in rags, moving along a path, and then the camera pulls back to show masses of people trudging across the landscape towards Lear's castle. Kozintsev makes it impossible to separate the play from the social experience that the drama represents and evaluates.

The culmination of the growth of Lear's understanding occurs when he wakes at Dover. He recognises Cordelia and assumes that his hostile actions will be repaid by her curse. She holds out the same relations of bond which got her banished in the first place. This establishes for Lear (who now has nothing else to confuse him) the primacy of personal relations. It is established *dramatically* in Act V, scene iii, in the interchange between

Cordelia and Lear, where he expresses the supreme importance of personal relations:

> Come, let's away to prison;
> We two alone will sing like birds i'th'cage:
> When thou dost ask me blessing, I'll kneel down,
> And ask of thee forgiveness: so we'll live,
> And pray, and sing, and tell old tales, and laugh
> At gilded butterflies, and hear poor rogues
> Talk of court news; and we'll talk with them too,
> Who loses and who wins; who's in, who's out;
> And take upon's the mystery of things,
> As if we were Gods' spies: and we'll wear out,
> In a wall'd prison, packs and sects of great ones
> That ebb and flow by th'moon. (V.iii.8–19)

This statement is constructed as Lear's and Cordelia's single victory over the monsters of individualism: they have lost, are captive, but have rediscovered each other – their *real* selves, not ceremonial images – and hold this more important than the hostile world around them. It is also for Lear the culmination of his whole learning process, the conclusion arrived at in a lifetime's experience. When Lear enters with his murdered daughter in his arms later in the scene, the anguish he expresses is at the destruction of someone else, not just his own loss.

> Why should a dog, a horse, a rat, have life,
> And thou no breath at all? Thou'lt come no more,
> Never, never, never, never, never! (V.iii.305–7)

The organisation of the action that gives dramatic emphasis to Lear's loss, as well as the intense concreteness of the poetry, heightens the sense of the importance of personal relationships, showing the world to be meaningless without them.

The personal relationships of which Lear and Cordelia are the model are, as it were, the 'bottom line' of humanity. This is the positive embodiment in the play of the substance of the 'need' that is not subject to rational calculation. It is the relationship of 'bond', of a recognised shared humanity, and a trust that makes that relationship sure and firm without needing (or being able to tolerate) contract or force.

This principle of mutuality and trust can be seen more clearly

from its contrary. When Goneril drives Lear out with the demand
that he halve his retinue, Albany suggests, in his distant, superior
manner, that she may be over-reacting. She replies with a manic
irony:

> This man hath had good counsel. A hundred knights!
> 'Tis politic and safe to let him keep
> At point a hundred knights; yes, that on every dream,
> Each buzz, each fancy, each complaint, dislike,
> He may enguard his dotage with their powers,
> And hold our lives in mercy. (I.iv.321–6)

Albany says, 'Well, you may fear too far', to which Goneril
answers:

> Safer than trust too far.
> Let me still take away the harms I fear,
> Not fear still to be taken. (I.iv.327–9)

The principle on which Goneril operates is clearly her own
well-being – reasonable enough – but without accommodating
any social view. This everyday sort of negation of social value
ultimately negates social relations. Why should we have *any* trust
if trust is a fool's game? Mutuality, shared humanity, personal,
non-contractual relations become impossible; the well of social
feeling is poisoned by the self-seeking, mistrusting individualist
because people, prey to others' selfishness, are forced into
'reasoning' a contradiction between protection of personal interests and participation in the richness of social relations. This is the
significance of Albany's 'monsters of the deep' (IV.ii.50). They *do*
indeed prey on each other, recognising no kind (i.e., the species
principle where one genus preys on others but not on its own),
but they are also monstrosities – denied the humanity that can
come only from society. This is a traditional view, perhaps
manifested earliest in Western culture by the image of the
Cyclops, a humanoid monster who lives in isolation. The single
eye is the physical manifestation of the monstrosity of the cyclops
but the significance is their alienation, their asocial being.
'Monsters of the *deep*', with its sense of separation in the dark
depths of the sea, intensifies the isolated image. If conduct like
Cornwall's tearing out of Goucester's eyes is not avenged by

heaven, Albany says, then humanity will turn monstrous; the monstrosity is the consequence of the individualistic attitudes of Goneril and Regan and Edmund.

But this leads to the matter of *King Lear* as a tragic structure, a question that, though it may appear purely formal, concerns the construction of social significance in Shakespeare's plays. Before approaching the social reverberations of form, it would make sense to expand on the development of the social argument and consider its first statement in *Hamlet*.

CHAPTER III

Hamlet

If *Hamlet* is viewed from the perspective of *King Lear*, the balance of attention shifts from the melancholic hero toward the playworld in which he moves, from questions of motive to the problem of grasping what reality really is. This re-orientation does not exclude other definitions of the content – the on-going disagreements over what the play is about are in part due to the fact that it *is* about so many things – but when Shakespeare based *Hamlet* on a revenge narrative that had already been made into a popular play only a few years before,[1] he must have found in his source something new that touched the concerns of the audience.

Hamlet is a new direction in Shakespeare's dramaturgy. Although some of his most popularly orientated entertainment had already touched on the conflict between tradition-directed and individualistic attitudes (the Second History Cycle and *King John*), *Hamlet* is the first play where this conflict becomes the central, and a tragic, concern. Although Shakespeare must have experienced such technical problems as occur with any prototype, probably more importantly, the subject matter was still in the process of definition and presented conceptual difficulties that are part of the complexity of the play. Even though the dramatic organisation orientates an audience in favour of some characters and against others, the principles on which the choices rest are not articulated. Traditional definitions *become* unclear as the

---

[1] Thomas Lodge, in his *Wits Miserie and the Worlds Madnesse*, 1596, uses *Hamlet*'s ghost as an index: Hate-Vertue 'looks as pale as the Visard of the ghost which cried so miserably at the Theator like an oisterwife, Hamlet, revenge . . .' sig.H4ᵛ. The comparison could be meaningful for an audience only if the play was well known to them.

reality of the play is made more complex, descriptive language turns out to be unreliable and the attitudes Shakespeare builds into the speeches and action are themselves confused, for *Hamlet* is genuinely exploratory.

The playworld of Elsinore is not a simple picture of disorder. Although there are images of both order and disorder presented from the beginning of the play, they are interwoven in a complex manner. Claudius has been legitimately elected king, he has formally married Gertrude with the approval of the courtiers, and he seems to rule efficiently; however, the procedures by which he has attained his present position (even though no one else yet knows about the murder) seem somewhat dubious. Protocols have been abused: the election of the king seems to have been carried out with undue haste, the wedding was indecently close to the funeral and the marriage is presented as technically incestuous.

Yet life at Court carries on as if all were normal. The first view of it, in the second scene, shows the king giving a long, ordered resume of the preceding events, instructing and dispatching ambassadors, giving a personal touch to his granting permission for Laertes to return to France, and further dealing with family matters in trying to persuade Hamlet to end his extended mourning. Claudius conveys order in his rhetoric. His balanced phrases, alliteration, end-stopped lines and contrived oxymorons resolve contradictions into the sense of a higher unity, as when he says Denmark is 'contracted in one brow of woe'. Nevertheless, in the first scene the theme was disorder, the appearance of a ghost, in a context of disrupted harmony between nature and society such that preparation for war 'Doth make the night joint-labourer with the day' (I.i.81)

In the life of the Court it is Hamlet, rather than the ghost or Claudius, who appears as the disruptive element. He disturbs the order of nature as well, persisting in mourning his father beyond the customary period, and his replies to Claudius and Gertrude are strikingly brief, one-liners that constitute a stylistic disruption, a rudeness in the midst of rhetorical graciousness comparable to Cordelia's 'nothing'. Thus when Gertrude echoes Claudius's rhetorical pattern, stressing to her son the naturalness of death –

> Good Hamlet, cast thy nighted colour off,
> And let thine eye look like a friend on Denmark.
> Do not for ever with thy vailed lids
> Seek for thy noble father in the dust.
> Thou know'st 'tis common: all that lives must die,
> Passing through nature to eternity. (I.ii.68–73)

– his response is curt: 'Ay, madam, it is common' (I.ii.74). Technically, Hamlet agrees with her, but only at the literal level. Stylistically he contradicts Gertrude, opposing the devices and elaboration of Court rhetoric with simple directness. Whereas in *Julius Caesar* Brutus and Cassius confront each other with rational argument, negotiate their positions, qualify each other's responses, etc. (as in the confrontation over how funds are raised to pay the soldiers in Act IV, scene iii, or among the conspirators in Brutus's garden in Act II, scene i), *Hamlet* follows quite a different pattern: Hamlet does not engage in reasoned discussion with his opponents but discredits their rhetoric through stylistic means. Distinguishing between 'seeming' and true being, he invalidates the rhetoric of the Court and introduces criteria for reality that are more immediate and more material. Claudius has the appearance of a competent ruler; he manipulates received opinion effectively and is *plausible* – until, or unless, the context is altered. The order of the Court is dramatically destabilised by Hamlet – for the audience at least, even if not for the Court itself.

The pattern of natural order invoked by Claudius and Gertrude exists, from the first lines of the play, in the context of a disorder more material than the appearance of the ghost (which is anyway insubstantial at the literal level): the sentries are confused about the most basic element of their guard role, who is the guard and who the challenger:

> *Barnardo.* Who's there?
> *Francisco.* Nay, answer me. Stand and unfold yourself.
> (I.i.1–2)

Unlike the world of *King Lear*, where the conflict is between clearly defined opposing systems, there is no such clarity in *Hamlet*. Rather, the existence of a standard is taken for granted without it being articulated, and it is against this assumed standard that the conduct of the present is measured. Without a clear standard, objective evaluation is not possible; the past becomes the repository of the goodness lacking in the present and judgement becomes nostalgia, an emotional index of the present degeneration. This process can be seen in the emblem of Hamlet comparing the miniatures of two kings for his mother's benefit:

> Look here upon this picture, and on this,
> The counterfeit presentment of two brothers.
> See what a grace was seated on this brow,
> Hyperion's curls, the front of Jove himself,
> An eye like Mars to threaten and command,
> A station like the herald Mercury
> New-lighted on a heaven-kissing hill,
> A combination and a form indeed
> Where every god did seem to set his seal
> To give the world assurance of a man.
> This was your husband. Look you now what follows.
> Here is your husband, like a mildew'd ear
> Blasting his wholesome brother. Have you eyes?
>   (III.iv.53–65)

Hamlet's comparison is made up entirely of subjective elements – 'an eye like Mars' opposed to a 'mildew'd ear' – but the judgement is assumed also to be objective: it is a quality that is felt, yet supposedly obvious to any observer. Hamlet senior and Claudius are superficially, technically, made to be functionally the same – 'your husband' – but, without the reasons for it being precisely defined, Claudius is depicted by Hamlet as a terrible decline from Hamlet senior.

The sense of the deterioration is that although the forms that once directed society still direct it, they have now lost their meaning; they have degenerated to being mere forms. This is seen most obviously in Hamlet's aggressive response to Gertrude's attempt to persuade him from his mourning, his 'seeming' speech. He responds not to the question Gertrude intends – why should he regard his own case of mourning as special? – but to her word 'seems'. The forms of showing grief cannot, he says, 'denote me truly':

> These indeed seem,
> For they are actions that a man might play;
> But I have that within which passes show,
> These but the trappings and the suits of woe.
>   (I.ii.83–6)

This appearance–reality distinction in matters of feeling may well have been a topos, a commonplace, by the time Shakespeare wrote – Sidney's sonnet 54 in *Astrophel and Stella* expresses quite clearly the confusion of form and feeling where Astrophel, because he does not follow lovers' form, is incorrectly assumed not to be a lover:

> Because I breathe not love to everie one,
>   Nor do not use set colours for to weare,
>   Nor nourish speciall lockes of vowed haire,
> Nor give each speech a full point of a grone,
> The courtly Nymphs, acquainted with the mone
>   Of them, who in their lips *Love's* standerd beare,
>   'What he?' say they of me, 'now I dare sweare,
> He cannot love: no, no, let him alone.'

Hamlet's speech also energetically attacks posing, the abandonment of the emotional content but retention of the form; he will not participate in hollow gesture.

A similar degeneration of function into empty form is given a comic presentation when Polonius gives fatherly advice to the departing Laertes. The twenty-odd lines of maxims for conduct are sound enough, but truisms gain no intellectual dignity just because they are true. The manner of presentation – cramming so many proverbial directions into a farewell – makes them impossible to assimilate and thus they become useless and ridiculous. And even though Polonius is amusing here – another humorous topos of the age, the senex-counsellor – the divergence of form and content becomes increasingly painful and serious.

Honour presents another area of decline. The noble Fortinbras fights for honour and has something noble in his style that appeals to Hamlet. Fortinbras, whom he describes as 'a delicate and tender prince', provides the model according to which

Hamlet berates himself for insufficiently bloody thinking and prompts him to the reflection:

> Rightly to be great
> Is not to stir without great argument,
> But greatly to find quarrel in a straw
> When honour's at the stake. (IV.iv.48, 53–6)

The lack of calculation is attractive; it is the opposite of the self-interest of the Court and the 'great argument' of financial gain. But it has also degenerated into reckless and pointless engagements, like Hal's caricature of Hotspur, 'he that kills me some six or seven dozen of Scots at a breakfast, washes his hands, and says to his wife, "Fie upon this quiet life, I want work"' (1 *Henry IV*, II.iv.100–3). The whole encounter shows the practical futility of Fortinbras's type of behaviour (20,000 men 'fight for a plot / Whereon the numbers cannot try the cause' – IV.iv.62–3). Hamlet, asking the Captain the nature of the military movement, suggests that it must have some purpose – 'against the main of Poland, sir, / Or for some frontier?' (IV.iv.15–16). When told that it is an almost worthless piece of ground, 'That hath in it no profit but the name' (IV.iv.19), he concludes – again, rational but mistaken – that it will not be defended. He utters a judgement of this great expenditure of life and substance for something of no value:

> This is th'impostume of much wealth and peace,
> That inward breaks, and shows no cause without
> Why the man dies. (IV.iv.27–9)

This is the pursuit of honour at the expense of social well-being; the social role has been driven out by individualism and honour is reduced to form. It is no longer the use of military power to protect people, but senseless destruction, without material or social gain, the hollow invocation of social honour for personal glory.

This, too, is a standard theme of the period, complained of, satirised or attacked by numerous Elizabethan writers. It is not just the notion of it being a 'leaden age', degenerated from the ages of nobler metals that preceded it. Sidney, for example, in *The Arcadia* makes fun of behaviour that is reduced to mere form and also develops the potential seriousness of such conduct in the civil war initiated and sustained by Amphialus. Nashe attacks social pretension and mannerisms practised to suggest honour in *Pierce Penniless* and also in *The Unfortunate Traveller*. And Thomas Deloney, almost as a corollary of his praise of industry, mocks people of rank who reduce honour from honourable conduct to mere style.

Hamlet does not provide Shakespeare's first discussion of this theme; he treated it at length in his Second History Cycle and *King John*. The honourable but outmoded Hotspur displays an individualistic conception of honour comparable to that of Fortinbras: it would be easy 'to pluck bright honour from the pale-fac'd moon' or, from bottomless depths, to 'pluck up drowned honour by the locks' if he could 'wear/ Without corrival all her dignities' (1 *Henry IV*, I.iii.200, 203, 204–5). Falstaff is the most obvious purveyor of degenerated form, the knight who fills the inherited forms of chivalry with a new individualistic content, and who reasons that honour is no more than a word because he can find no material reality for it (1 *Henry IV*, V.i.129–41). But Falstaff is presented clearly and unquestionably as disreputable, which dissociates him from any admiration on Shakespeare's part; nevertheless his attitudes infect the hero and it is from Falstaff that Hal has learned how to interpret the world.

In *Hamlet* the slippage between the customary meaning of the form and the actual content is more serious because the problem is endemic, not localised in particular individuals. And whereas the Second History Cycle displays it piecemeal, it is in effect the subject matter of *Hamlet*.

Relocating the villainy

The problem of Hamlet's world is rampant individualism. In the inherited story Shakespeare used and in his own plot the problem is the villain, Claudius, who is a murderer and usurper – *Hamlet* is a revenge play. But in the way Shakespeare elaborates the basic plot, his selection of material and the choice of scenes to present, the problem is clearly broader than that. Hamlet's dissatisfaction with the world, his critique of the shortcomings of his society, his melancholy are made clear from the start, before the call for revenge. Claudius is by no means isolated in his selfish and anti-social attitudes, although he may be the most spectacular instance of rampant individualism. His criminality is different only in degree, not in kind, from the behaviour of numerous other quasi-villains in the play, and his attitudes are the rule rather than the exception. He diverges from 'the normal' only a little more than, say, Laertes, whose normality is only slightly less than that of Osric. Behaviour that dispenses with trust and integrity is not in the least remarked.

Polonius offers a clear instance of the degeneration of the content of social forms. He moves through the play with the dignity (or at least pretension to it) of a Lord Chancellor but his practice contradicts it. While his dignity perhaps can withstand the mockery of Hamlet calling him a fishmonger and being made to identify cloud shapes, his behaviour in his role as parent discredits him more seriously. In Act I, scene iii, his frivolous questioning of Laertes turns into a serious interrogation of Ophelia about her relationship with Hamlet, the subject of her earlier discussion with Laertes. Polonius enters on this interchange already having assumed the conventional character of the senex, the foolish old man, from the string of apophthegms to which he subjected Laertes; but the directed character of the dialogue with Ophelia (and what eventually becomes clear as its importance for the plot) give it a steely edge. Polonius acquires substance and his 'normality' becomes dangerous. Unlike the contrived situations in which mockery of authority usually takes place (as in Hamlet's engagement with Polonius in the fishmonger scene or a similar construction from *Measure for Measure*, where Lucio mocks the Duke), Polonius is the one who controls the interchange and thus his conduct is more revealing.

The encounter presents little information and the agreement reached (that Ophelia will not see Hamlet) has neither the development nor complexity to justify the length of discussion. What we are given is an exercise of power seen in the way the language is used. Thus Polonius, at the mention of Hamlet, begins to lecture Ophelia, and even though he speaks only hypothetically of the intensity of their relationship ('If it be so'), he draws the conclusion before the facts are established – 'You do not understand yourself so clearly/ As it behoves my daughter and your honour' (I.iii.96–7). In asking for Ophelia's response he insults her, suggesting at the same time that she might incline toward lying: 'What is between you? Give me up the truth' (l.98).

Worse than the suggestion of lying, Polonius devalues everything Ophelia says, treating her as stupidly naive and, from the beginning, humiliating her. When she says that Hamlet has 'of late made many tenders/ Of his affection to me' (ll.99–100), Polonius immediately questions 'affection' and then casts doubt on whether 'tenders' has any real meaning: 'Do you believe his tenders, as you call them?' (l.103). Ophelia, clearly placed on the wrong foot, does not answer directly but, retreating from the positive statement of her preceding speech, in effect asks what it is that he wants of her, which is his cue to lecture her. He belittles her, by calling her a baby and making a self-indulgent, punning mockery of her word 'tender'

At Polonius's mention of possible consequences of the relationship, 'you'll tender me a fool' (a suggestion that Ophelia's credulity, or foolishness, will lead to her getting pregnant, which will affect Polonius's own honour), Ophelia makes her one protest: 'My lord, he hath importun'd me with love/ In honourable fashion' (ll.110–11). She even counters Polonius's hostile rejoinder – 'Ay, fashion you may call it' – by insisting on Hamlet's 'holy vows' (ll.112, 114). Polonius then launches into a lengthy rejection of the possibility that love is the motive of the relationship, saying that it is only lust that motivates Hamlet and leads him (as it did the young Polonius himself) to false swearing:

Ay, springes to catch woodcocks. I do know,
When the blood burns, how prodigal the soul
Lends the tongue vows. (I.iii.115–17)

He moves from the generality of young men to Hamlet, telling Ophelia not to believe him, forbidding her to see him.

Ophelia has been crushed by Polonius; she answers only 'I shall obey, my lord' (l.136).

This interchange has a causal function in the plot. The Prince appears before Ophelia in the posture of the distracted lover – 'with his doublet all unbrac'd', 'his stockings foul'd', 'And with a look so piteous in purport/ As if he had been loosed out of hell'

(II.i.78, 79, 82–3). The space Shakespeare allows description here makes it more than form: not just unfortunate in his love, Hamlet has been betrayed by Ophelia. This appears in the bitterness he expresses toward her for 'selling out' in the 'Get thee to a nunnery' interview (III.i) and before the play-within-a-play (III.ii). Such a hostile rejection must in turn contribute to her own madness. But the plot function alone could have been achieved without the detail of the interchange. Shakespeare is characterising the atmosphere of Elsinore and showing the slippage between form and content. Polonius acts the part of the careful father, mindful of the dangers that beset his young daughter and concerned to protect her; but the actual content of his behaviour is patriarchal arrogance and the mangling of his daughter's feelings and self-image. Shakespeare does not have available a terminology that recognises the difference between the real content of this behaviour and its abstract definition – Polonius's role can be defined here as a 'father' – and therefore he must show the behaviour concretely to reveal the contradictions between the image and the actuality. Abstract language is not sufficiently flexible to reveal the reality; in the manner of Lear learning the meanings of father and daughter, Shakespeare offers the understanding through concrete experience.

Even though Polonius admits he was wrong about Hamlet and Ophelia –

> I am sorry that with better heed and judgment
> I had not quoted him. I fear'd he did but trifle
> And meant to wrack thee. But beshrew my jealousy!

– he does not display any concern for his responsibility for the consequences of his acts, because he was only doing what everyone else does:

> By heaven, it is as proper to our age
> To cast beyond ourselves in our opinions
> As it is common for the younger sort
> To lack discretion. (II.i.111–13, 114–17)

It is this complacency he sees around him that is the aspect of corruption at Elsinore that Hamlet perhaps finds most provocative. It is not just that bad deeds are committed, but that those who commit them fail, or are unwilling, to recognise their badness. The problem is more than a naivety with vicious consequences (such as Beatrice-Joanna displays in *The Changeling* of Middleton) and ranges from an individualism that does not consider the consequences of actions to an acceptance of anything that promotes self-advancement. Thus Polonius again, at the beginning of the scene where Ophelia reports Hamlet's distraction, sets Reynaldo to spy on Laertes. He enjoys his own rhetoric –

> See you now,
> Your bait of falsehood takes this carp of truth;
> And thus do we of wisdom and of reach,
> With windlasses and with assays of bias,
> By indirections find directions out (II.i.62–6)

– but it is the verbal dexterity rather than the appropriateness that he attends to, even though Reynaldo briefly begins to raise objections ('My lord, that would dishonour him' and 'But my good lord –', II.ii.27, 36). Polonius, as with Ophelia, performs an act of some destructiveness while playing the role of the good father. Having his son spied on is not monstrous in the way that the crushing of Ophelia is, but it is a degeneration of a relationship which, in concept at least, should include a good measure of trust. Even though Polonius may appear a concerned parent and regard himself as a wise parent, the audience can at the least recognise an objectionable quality in his actions.

The interchange between Reynaldo and Polonius has no function in terms of plot: the information about Laertes's behaviour in Paris never surfaces in the play, Reynaldo does not return and no reference is made to the scene or situation again. Structurally then it is of no consequence, nor is it comic; its function is to characterise normality at Elsinore.

Laertes, given a less defined character and less to do in the plot than his father, is perhaps a more telling demonstration of the spread and unremarkableness of corruption at Elsinore. In his first appearance, making his farewells to Ophelia, he seems a rather shallow youth; he has a narrower perspective than his sister and is rather conventional, with his thinking caught in the abstract situation of a prince courting a woman of lesser rank, rather than attending to the actual relationship between his sister and Hamlet. There is no suggestion that he is potentially evil or destructive, no Reynaldo queries his actions; he seems a decent enough fellow.

Laertes is still in the conventional mould when he storms into the palace to avenge his father's death on Claudius, in Act IV, scene v:

> How came he dead? I'll not be juggled with.
> To hell, allegiance! Vows to the blackest devil!
> Conscience and grace, to the profoundest pit!
> I dare damnation. To this point I stand,
> That both the worlds I give to negligence,
> Let come what comes, only I'll be reveng'd
> Most throughly for my father. (IV.v.130–6)

He is the hot-headed revenger, vigorously pursuing a role the complexity of which has not occurred to him. Claudius works skilfully on this naivety in the next scene, directing the rage of Laertes to Hamlet and then urging it gradually beyond the bounds of decent hostility:

> *Claud.*   what would you undertake
> To show yourself in deed your father's
> More than in words?
> *Laertes.* To cut his throat i'th'church.
> *Claud.* No place indeed should murder sanctuarize;
> Revenge should have no bounds. (IV.vii.123–7)

Claudius says he will arrange a duel between Hamlet and Laertes where Laertes can treacherously kill the prince:

> you may choose
> A sword unbated, and in a pass of practice,
> Requite him for your father. (IV.vii.136–8)

Not only does Laertes accept the corrupted conditions of the match, he does not even object when Claudius refers to his killing Hamlet as 'a pass of practice', a treachery that would seem to destroy the potential nobility of the revenge. And Laertes further adds his own treachery:

> I will do't.
> And for that purpose, I'll anoint my sword.
> I bought an unction of a mountebank
> So mortal that but dip a knife in it,
> Where it draws blood, no cataplasm so rare,
> Collected from all simples that have virtue
> Under the moon, can save the thing from death
> That is but scratch'd withal. I'll touch my point
> With this contagion, that if I gall him slightly,
> It may be death. (IV.vii.138–47)

Thus the noble revenger transforms himself into an underhanded poisoner, without any loss of self-respect. This is the noble youth well regarded by Elsinore. His behaviour is 'normal'.

The most telling naturalisation of corruption, the 'bottom line' of complacency, is the otherwise insignificant Osric. Osric is an ordinary courtier. His longest appearance is as the butt of Hamlet's wit when, with all the affectation of a fop, he bears Claudius's challenge to Hamlet. The most striking characteristic of the interchange between the two is probably the affectation and incomprehensibility of Osric's language (rich matter to stimulate footnotes). Hamlet seems the only person capable of understanding it, but he is forced to ask what Osric means by 'carriages' of swords and Horatio says, 'I knew you must be edified by the margin ere you had done' (V.ii.152–3). Osric's language has degenerated to being mere decoration; the actuality of the referents fades and no meaningful reality remains. The meaning is in the style; it is trendy, fashionable, and anyone who does not use it is marked as an outsider.

Yet Hamlet's attitude seems more hostile than mere foppishness would warrant:

> . . . for 'tis a vice to know him. He hath much land and fertile. Let a beast be lord of beasts and his crib shall stand at the king's mess. 'Tis a chuff, but, as I say, spacious in the possession of dirt. (V.ii.85–9)

It is the vehemence of his dislike that makes the interchange serious and prevents the excessive language from being comic, as is the wordplay of the gravediggers. The hostility is justified by Osric's function, for, as referee in Hamlet's duel with Laertes,

Osric is the agent of murder, arranging for Laertes to take the unbated sword. He is, in effect, Laertes's accomplice. He lacks individualising traits, his language is without personal character – he is the most ordinary character in the play – and yet he is distinctly a villain.

Unlike the phrase-mongering of Holofernes and Armado in *Love's Labour's Lost*, Osric presents a linguistic embodiment of the corruption that Hamlet faces. And since language transmits and orders values, Osric's behaviour suggests that its corruption is connected with that of the state. His behaviour is unconcernedly murderous, a reality that can easily disappear behind his meaningless language. The problem is not that he uses language to *disguise* his meaning (in the manner of, say, Edmund) but that the slippage of meaning allows him to escape personal responsibility. His language pretends to values he does not himself hold and anyone who says, for example, 'an absolute gentleman, full of most excellent differences, of very soft society and great showing' (V.ii.107–8), means too little to be held responsible for any consequences. Osric is very much at home in the complacency of the Court. The role language plays for Osric, even though Shakespeare does not stress it, gives force of principle to Cordelia's refusal to abuse language in a seemingly innocent way to flatter her father.

The most significant complacency in the play is Gertrude's, which is the theme of the 'closet' scene. Hamlet's behaviour is from the opening of the scene decidedly rude; Gertrude is the Queen, not just his mother, and he contradicts what she says and mocks her:

> *Queen.* Hamlet, thou hast thy father much offended.
> *Hamlet.* Mother, you have my father much offended.
> *Queen.* Come, come, you answer with an idle tongue.
> *Hamlet.* Go, go, you question with a wicked tongue.
>   (III.iv.8–11)

Hamlet appears hostile – 'You are the Queen, your husband's brother's wife,/ And, would it were not so, you are my mother' (III.iv.14–15) – to such an extent that when in his next speech he utters the ambiguous lines

Come, come, and sit you down, you shall not budge.
You go not till I set you up a glass
Where you may see the inmost part of you (III.iv.17–19)

the Queen (perhaps understanding the lines literally) thinks he is
going to attack her: 'What wilt thou do? Thou wilt not murder
me?' (III.iv.20). Gertrude recognises the violence of Hamlet's
emotion but can see no cause for it, and thus reasonably assumes
that it constitutes a threat to herself; i.e., Hamlet appears to be
having a fit of violent rage, unrelated to any conduct she can
understand but which he obviously fixes on her.

T. S. Eliot, in his essay on *Hamlet* (where he introduces the
famous 'objective correlative'), shares Gertrude's misunderstanding. He says that Hamlet's anger is obvious, and directed at
Gertrude, but the play does not show anything she has done to
deserve such anger: she 'is not an adequate equivalent for it; his
disgust envelops and exceeds her'.[2] The drama of this confrontation Shakespeare probably derives from Richard Johnson's
popular fiction of 1599, *Tom a Lincoln, the Red-Rose Knight.*
Johnson, however, is more interested in the action itself than its
significance. In his work, the son (the Black Knight) confronts
his mother who has been living in an adulterous relationship with
the Knight of the Castle. When her husband, the Red-Rose
Knight, finally discovers her, she joins her lover in killing him.
The son has no qualms about killing the Knight of the Castle,
which he does without delay, but his mother kneels before him in
her smock and pleads for her life, saying 'wound not the wombe
that fostred thee'. He has a moment of doubt ('I am almost
strucke with remorce') but, when the angry ghost of his father
appears before him, he kills her with his sword (ed. Richard S. M.
Hirsch, 1978, University of South Carolina Press, Columbia, p.
83). Anglitora (the Gertrude figure) was guilty in the obvious,
admitted way of Richard III, whereas in *Hamlet* the facts
themselves are of less importance than their integration into
patterns of behaviour, which gives them significance.

The same thing can be seen clearly in a brief interchange, when

---

[2] T. S. Eliot, '*Hamlet*' (1919), in *Selected Prose of T. S. Eliot*, ed. Frank
Kermode (1975: Faber & Faber, London), p. 48.

Polonius tells Claudius he has discovered 'The very cause of Hamlet's lunacy' (II.ii.49). Shakespeare underlines the exchange and gives importance to the matter by repeating it. The repetition is not required by the context in which the communication occurs – Claudius and Gertrude are presumably sitting next to each other and she can hear Polonius – so Claudius telling her what Polonius has just told him is for the benefit of the audience. He says:

> He tells me, my dear Gertrude, he hath found
> The head and source of all your son's distemper

to which she replies:

> I doubt it is no other but the main,
> His father's death and our o'er-hasty marriage.
> (II.ii.54–7)

Gertrude's judgement is probably accurate here; the problem is her 'no other but', her easy acceptance of the situation, her complacency.

In the remainder of the closet scene, after he has slain Polonius, Hamlet attacks Gertrude's complacency and makes her feel guilty:

> O Hamlet, speak no more.
> Thou turn'st my eyes into my very soul,
> And there I see such black and grained spots
> As will not leave their tinct. (III.iv.88–91)

But they do not arrive at a mutual understanding; he sees the ghost and she does not, and she assumes therefore that he is mad, a theatrical rendering of their different understanding. In the conclusion of the scene she agrees not to repeat what he has said ('Be thou assur'd, if words be made of breath,/ And breath of life, I have no life to breathe/ What thou hast said to me.' – ll.199–201) but she now seems to have lost the sense of contrition she had earlier displayed. However justified Hamlet's anger at Gertrude, in his railing against her choice of second husband and her middle-aged sensuality, his sexual disgust is rendered so intensely that it does not allow the corruption he attacks to be seen in more general terms. The specific theme of sexual corruption recurs frequently in Shakespeare's work. In what is probably the most notable passage, Lear's attack on luxury – women who are centaurs below the waist, whose civilised air conceals a rank, corrupt lust (IV.vi.116–28) – it is selfish, anti-social behaviour that is objected to, something quite different from the 'socialised' sexuality that ends happily in marriage, such as that of Rosalind. In any case, Hamlet has not succeeded in shaking her complacency.

Hamlet and revenge

The problem of Hamlet's revenge, his delay, is related to his perception of the complacency of the Court. Revenge is more than someone establishing an equality of hostile actions – tit for tat; it is a complex cultural form. The action must fulfil the basic requirement of producing pain at least equal to the original injury, but it must also be of a definite character, in keeping with the way Bacon characterised it – 'a kind of wild justice' (*The Essays*, ed. J. Pitcher, 1985, Penguin, Harmondsworth, p. 77.).

In Thomas Nashe's *The Unfortunate Traveller*, Cutwolfe, 'a wearish dwarfish writhen-faced cobbler', makes a speech relating the course of his vengeance, before he is broken on the wheel (ed. J. B. Steane, 1972, Penguin, Harmondsworth, pp. 363–9). What gives this description particular value is that, because it is a public execution, we are given 'audience response' to Cutwolfe's story, as well as commentary by Jack Wilton, the book's narrator. Nashe thus provides an excellent picture of the Elizabethan concept of revenge: the victim must not only suffer but also know the reason for it, and the punishment should be appropriate to the original injury. Thus Medea takes revenge on Jason, her faithless husband, through a wedding gift that destroys his new wife and by murdering Jason's and her own children; Hieronymo of *The Spanish Tragedy*, in a love drama that parodies the original crime, slays those who have murdered his son, bringing incurable anguish to their parents, who are also peripherally guilty. The intense satisfaction of revenge depends on its 'rightness', which is an aesthetic counterpart of justice. Before Cutwolfe kills Esdras of Granado he must be sure that he feels his guilt, without which the revenge would seem to be arbitrary.

Hamlet is faced with a killer who is legally guilty but whose behaviour is generally condoned by the Court. The courtiers might balk at regicide but they can remain happy in their ignorance. For Hamlet to take revenge, then, even if he is prompted to it by heaven and hell, would seem to violate, rather than restore, order at Elsinore – it is contrary to the social reality. Claudius is not an obvious criminal and is in a supportive environment where his values are shared; Hamlet must be assured that Claudius actually *feels* guilt before killing him.

While the 'mousetrap' in the play Shakespeare inherited would seem to have functioned to reveal the King as a murderer, for Shakespeare's hero its success seems to lie in bringing Claudius's sense of wrong-doing to the surface: his upset is an expression of feeling guilty. (The argument over whether the ghost is 'honest' or not has substance only in analysis; dramatically, there has been no doubt cast by the play on the ghost's validity.) Hamlet's manic delight that overflows when the King leaves the performance is his sense of victory, of having manoeuvred Claudius into a position where he is ripe for vengeance. Hamlet's 'delay', required by the inherited plot, is justified by his waiting for an appropriate moment, when the King also *appears* worthy of vengeance – which clearly is not when he is at prayers. Such a moment, given the complacency of the Court, is an unlikely occurrence, but a revenge that is not 'objectively' justified, that is comprehensible to only himself and Horatio, is useless to Hamlet. The delay makes sense in those terms but it means that, finally, Hamlet's revenge is only technically a success.

The instance of successful revenge that Shakespeare offers in the play is Hamlet's arranging the deaths of Rosencrantz and Guildenstern. When the balanced Horatio says, 'So Guildenstern and Rosencrantz go to't' (V.ii.56), it raises possible uneasiness that Hamlet's revenge is too sharp, but Shakespeare has Hamlet vigorously affirm its appropriateness:

Why, man, they did make love to this employment.
They are not near my conscience, their defeat
Does by their own insinuation grow. (V.ii.57–9)

They willingly participated in the corruption of the Court, betraying Hamlet for personal advancement while still calling themselves his friends. They deserved everything they got and there is pleasure for an audience in the justice, as well as the sport, of Hamlet delving 'one yard below their mines' and having 'the enginer hoist with his own petard' (III.iv.210,208–9).

Hamlet's comments in regard to the death of Polonius similarly make a judgement on his character, and Polonius is denied any possibility of tragic dignity. Whereas Hal speaks heroically of the dead Hotspur he mocked while he was alive – 'When that this body did contain a spirit,/ A kingdom for it was too small a bound' (1 *Henry IV*, V.iv.88–9), Hamlet mocks the dead Polonius, dragging 'the guts' from the room and pronouncing the lines that are Polonius's dramatic epitaph:

> This counsellor
> Is now most still, most secret, and most grave,
> Who was in life a foolish prating knave. (III.iv.215–17)

He continues the mockery when brought before Claudius, three scenes later, by telling the king Polonius is at supper, 'Not where he eats, but where a is eaten. A certain convocation of politic worms are e'en at him' (IV.iii.19–20).

As Ophelia, besieged by his manic hostility as they watch the 'mousetrap', says of Hamlet, he is 'keen' (III.ii.243); his world is falling apart and it would seem he can do nothing about it.

The problem of definition

Even if Eliot's aesthetic outlook makes him fail to see the cause of Hamlet's anger, he recognises that Shakespeare's fundamental difficulty in *Hamlet* was finding a way of expressing what was not yet clear to him. For Eliot to say, 'the play is most certainly an artistic failure' (ibid, p. 47), is extreme but not entirely without justification. Not only is the problem of definition of good and bad, at one level, the subject matter of the play, but *Hamlet* itself posed for Shakespeare an almost insuperable problem of definition. If social practice changes and the words that mark that practice either do not change or change at a different rate, then a model of the world constructed from language will inevitably be frustrated by the actuality. This is most obvious in language that reflects the natural world; 'the four corners of the earth' offers a linguistic model of the world that could only frustrate geographical investigation. The problem is infinitely more complex when words are used to signal moral qualities. As Feste says in *Twelfth Night* (a play contemporary with *Hamlet* and in some ways offering a comic treatment of overlapping themes), 'they that dally nicely with words may quickly make them wanton' (III.i.14–15).

The paradoxical nature of immaterial words with material referents is a traditional topic. What distinguishes Shakespeare's use of it perhaps is that it is accompanied by a bitterness that may not have been present before, the same bitterness that characterises Lear's understanding that the goal-posts have been moved and the rules changed. The value scheme represented in the language applied to the Court was no longer operative, yet it continued to be part of the language used. This means that the representations of material reality in language were inadequate. This is not a matter of irony, or meaning the direct opposite of what the words literally convey, but a slippage between word and referent, where expectation remains with the word but is frustrated in life. This is different from the brutal double meaning of Richard's words of seeming comfort to Clarence in the second scene of *Richard III* – 'Well, your imprisonment shall not be long: / I will deliver you, or else lie for you' (I.i.114–15) – or the juggling of the witches' words to Macbeth that he need not fear till Burnham wood comes to Dunsinane. It has more the character of the almost contemporary *Julius Caesar* where Antony's 'Brutus is an honourable man' (III.ii.87) means more than he is not really honourable and raises the whole question of what honour actually is, in a way far more consequential than Falstaff's sophistical destruction of the term.

In practical terms, those in *Hamlet* who occupied the positions to which certain social values were traditionally attached no longer held those values. Thus the image of a king, what a king means in the social fabric which the language reflects, is presented most clearly in Shakespeare's work by Macbeth's reflections on what Duncan is like and the reasons he should not kill him – 'this Duncan/ Hath borne his faculties so meek, hath been/ So clear in his great office' (I.vii.16–18), etc. – and by Hamlet's own picture of his father as king, a man of noble judgement, passionless wisdom, elevated impartiality, unquestionable dignity and selfless commitment to tradition-sanctioned common weal. The reality is presented by a man who has alienated himself from those qualities, by Claudius – 'remorseless, treacherous, lecherous, kindless villain'. The same word 'king' is applied to both. At the level of the word, the verbal signifier, they are interchangeable (and also in various symbols such as the miniatures of 'the king' that both Hamlet and Gertrude carry, the one of his father and the other of Claudius), but the substance is very different.

The people of the Court are, in the terms of the period, gentlemen and women 'of worship'. 'Worship' (the same root as 'worth') means that they have qualities deserving of honour and esteem – they are worthy – and it also means they have a rank or position of honour. The second sense seems dependent on the first, in that the objective honour of rank assumes the presence of the personal honour. Subjective and objective are in harmony. To say, then, that a person has a position of 'worship' suggests that they have also the personal integrity – too obvious a contradiction between the two worships is socially unacceptable, in the same way that impoverished gentlefolk eventually are dropped from the roll of gentility. Claudius, Gertrude, Polonius, etc., all the villains and accomplices of the Court of Elsinore, are worshipful and yet they have no worship. The contradiction is a problem of definition: the reality has changed but the language has not, so the definition is inadequate to the reality.

Falstaff's subversive phrase, 'A pox of this gout! or a gout of this pox!', is a delightfully witty instance of this. (Lear's 'handy-dandy, which is the justice, which is the thief?', IV.vi.151–2, may be a weightier echo of the same thing.) But in *Hamlet* it is a serious matter. Rosencrantz and Guildenstern, for example, are 'friends', but their behaviour requires a redefinition of 'friendship'. Polonius is a 'concerned father', though his behaviour, as we have seen, conflicts sharply with the genuine parental concern.

It is as if Hamlet has to face the problem that the 'good guys' are the 'bad guys', but they are still called 'good guys'. It is disorientating not only because it is contrary to expectations, but also because it is nearly inexpressible. The basic elements of the value scheme are assumed without articulation, so the intellectual framework that would enable a clear differentiation to be made – that would supply terms and definitions – does not exist. In *Richard III* Richard is deceitful but there is no problem with definitions; he bounces on to the stage and says 'I am determined to prove a villain' (I.i.30), which confirms rather than challenges the audience's sense of good and bad. *Hamlet* suffers from vague areas, people for whom the definition is not replaced by its opposite but who fail to fulfil the qualities defined; good and bad have altered. Shakespeare has not yet objectified the change to the point where contradictions can be represented in language or given the concrete presentation in paradox, as in *King Lear* where the King of France speaks of Cordelia as 'this unpriz'd precious maid' (I.i.258), and in the highly developed paradoxical language of *Macbeth*. The frustration of an inadequate system of representing the world is part of Hamlet's rage, a rage for a whole society, not just himself.

The collapse of the assured points of existence is not merely a matter of the recognition of the changing reality; it is also a problem of language, the instrument that records and rearranges reality. The language continues to reflect fixed points of existence that are no longer there. Osric's overblown discourse, for example, is inadequate to the task of describing itself; it has no terms for the inflation and hollowness of which it is the chief example. It is like the Heisenberg Uncertainty Principle – the location and movement of atomic particles cannot be accurately measured because the process of measuring affects their velocity. The degenerated reality cannot be measured in the language that is one index of its degeneration. When Feste is asked his reason for saying, 'words are very rascals', he replies, 'I can yield you none without words, and words are grown so false, I am loath to prove reason with them' (*Twelfth Night*, III.i.20, 23–5). Even though the 'good guys' are no longer good, the statement that the 'good guys' are 'bad guys' is meaningless. Shakespeare is required to make the tools at the same time as he is making the product, a feat he attempts in *Hamlet*, with only partial success.

There are other aspects of the play that suggest Shakespeare had difficulties in making things clear, such as its length, the reliance on soliloquy to explain the difference of Hamlet's reality from that around him, the role of Horatio as confidant, etc. It is demonstrated in such interchanges as the closet scene and numerous occasions of Hamlet wilfully talking at cross purposes (e.g., 'I know not seems' or 'Lady, shall I lie in your lap?'). The interchange with Polonius as fishmonger, even though in some ways a very effective scene, illustrates Shakespeare's difficulty. The initial discussion, after a greeting, is about identity – 'Do you know me, my lord?' Hamlet says, 'Excellent well. You are a fishmonger.' Polonius of course fails to recognise this identity and denies it: 'Not I. my lord.' Hamlet then moves to generalisation, saying 'Then I would you were so honest a man', and explains further when Polonius voices his lack of understanding of 'honest', 'Ay sir. To be honest, as this world goes, is to be one man picked out of ten thousand.' Polonius agrees: 'That's very true, my lord' (II.ii.171–80). Hamlet and Polonius have arrived at a point of agreement but it is only superficial, in the words, for they have two opposed understandings of reality.

The discussion turns from identity to a particular aspect of it, 'honesty', a word Polonius might well see in its more archaic sense of honourable, respectable, decent, while Hamlet plays on the sense of straightforward, upright, sincere, truthful; and that would be sufficient reason for Polonius to be taken slightly aback when Hamlet wishes him as honest as a fishmonger. The argument becomes one of form and essence. Formally, it is ridiculous to see Polonius, the Chancellor, as a tradesman. This is part self-indulgent foolery on the part of Hamlet, and part identification of the essential Polonius as a bawd. A fishmonger relates to someone who keeps a stews, either a pond stocked with live fish that can be taken out for the table when desired or, metaphorically, a brothel. Polonius, in controlling the exercise of his daughter's affection for his own ends, is effectively a pimp, and thus fishmonger – but not openly, 'honestly' so. The matter of honour signalled in 'honest' is seen by Polonius in its formal aspect, his standing, whereas Hamlet is arguing an essentially dishonourable behaviour. Their agreement then is merely formal; at the essential level the differences remain unresolved.

The interchange is witty and amusing. It offers Hamlet the chance to get the better of Polonius, giving the audience the pleasure of witnessing that small victory, and it reinforces the contrast between the lively comprehension of the Prince and the tradition-bound dullness of the Lord Chancellor, but it hardly serves to advance the plot. Of the forty-nine lines of the exchange, twenty-six are given to Hamlet, twenty-three to Polonius. Hamlet's lines are all spoken directly to Polonius, but more than ten of Polonius's, nearly half his speech, are asides. The asides are humorous, showing Polonius's misunderstanding of what Hamlet is saying, but they also have the effect of soliloquy: they allow Polonius to make an uninterrupted presentation of his view of reality. The point here is that the opposition between the perspectives (not just the personalities) is not immediately clear by itself; Shakespeare needs to give Polonius the asides for it to be made clear. The problem is not that these perspectives are difficult to distinguish because they are close to each other (they are not); it is that their *articulation* is not yet highly developed. The clumsiness necessary to present the opposition is an indication of Shakespeare's difficulty, a difficulty which, it would seem, is reflected in the problem he gave to Hamlet.

The result of Shakespeare being only partly successful in articulating the difference of perspectives is that the play attracts the attention of audiences and readers more to the interesting consciousness of the hero than to the world in which he moves. The focus of attention, reasonably enough, becomes something concrete – the attitudes and psyche of the hero – rather than an indefinable (as it would seem to be here) reality. In keeping with critical attitudes that tend to represent literature as a private activity (and drama as literature), *Hamlet* is assumed to be a play about an individual, i.e., that the focus of Shakespeare's interest is the eponymous hero and the other elements of the play exist as background. With the notable exception of Grigori Kozintsev's film of the tragedy (USSR, 1964), this seems to be the case with most productions as well as in critical commentary. The hero's consciousness is essential, the most important focus of aesthetic energy in the play, but it is the *content* of that consciousness, not its psychological structure, that is important. *Hamlet* presents, rather than the exposition of a unique psyche, a picture of the late Elizabethan world viewed through the hero's eyes, the 'new' world heralded by the Second History Cycle, of opportunism and cynical self-interest. To attend to Hamlet's psyche only is to trivialise Shakespeare's vision.

Despite being profoundly moving, *Hamlet* remains somewhat unsatisfactory. Shakespeare's dependence on the consciousness of the hero for judgement of the playworld frustrates audience expectations of drama's objectification, of seeing it for themselves. Because the formalised understanding available in the play is like that of Polonius, tradition-bound and inhospitable to learning from actual experience, Shakespeare has no means of articulating values clearly; systematic understanding – ideology – in the play belongs to the 'enemy'. Shakespeare makes Hamlet carry alone the whole burden of opposition. Hamlet sees what is wrong but, as Arnold Kettle explained it in an exceptionally useful essay, without a coherent opposition, he can go no further than rejecting dominant ideas, recognising honour in the 'breach' without proposing an alternative.[3]

The gravediggers offer a sense of ultimate victory – the final justice of the skull beneath the skin, death the great equaliser that takes the rich and poor, fair and foul, upright and corrupt – but this is also the counterpart of recognising that real justice, in this world, is impossible. A semi-coherent view propounded by one character, in opposition to the habits of a whole society, is not a balance likely to be able to effect significant changes in the thinking of the audience. It is as if Hamlet were jumping up and down, pointing to the disaster of society, but attracting audience attention only to a very interesting person jumping up and down, to himself. Shakespeare needed something that could make his points objectively. In the years immediately following *Hamlet* he turned to a very different kind of drama, to work of pronounced artifice constructed in such a way as to produce clarity of understanding less than to make the audience uncomfortable. Then he found the solution to the structural and conceptual difficulties of *Hamlet* in *King Lear*.

[3] Arnold Kettle, 'From *Hamlet* to *Lear*', *Shakespeare in a Changing World: Essays on His Times and His Plays*, ed. Arnold Kettle (1964: Lawrence & Wishart, London).

CHAPTER IV

King Lear II

In *Hamlet* Shakespeare raised problems of representation that he was unable to solve in the play. Exactly what is being represented is not clear, nor is the point of the action evident from the course of action itself. The plot often does not convey adequately the issues of the play, and Shakespeare resorts to telling instead of showing, as in Hamlet's report of arranging the deaths of Rosencrantz and Guildenstern. There are interchanges of dramatic inefficiency, such as the single-function exchange between Polonius and Reynaldo, which provides a useful qualification of the nature of the playworld and the character of Polonius but is not integrated into the plot. The fishmonger exchange depends on Polonius's asides – in effect, his soliloquy – to make clear differences in perspective. Shakespeare relies heavily on soliloquies to convey the hero's orientation. Hamlet's soliloquies are certainly of outstanding poetic quality but they are not dramatic; they indicate a weakness in Shakespeare's construction. The play's very length suggests that it is aesthetically inefficient.

These shortcomings of *Hamlet*'s dramaturgy are important because they make it difficult for Shakespeare to establish meaning. The issues around which the play is centred are different from those that determine the course of the plot. Plot therefore does not direct understanding or control the attention of the audience effectively. Rather, audience attention focuses naturally on those aspects of the play that are most developed, where the greatest density of signals occurs – Hamlet's pain, his psychological complexity, the richness of his vision, etc. The result for many (perhaps most) people is that, instead of moving outward from the hero to the world he judges, attention remains on Hamlet himself. His judgements about social disintegration are reduced to attitudinising, their content regarded as of little importance, and the subject of his rage is ignored. If Hamlet's frustrations are to be understood as more than signals for emotion, if Shakespeare regards their specific content as important (which is suggested by the intensity of the play) then a structure not dependent on the perspective of a single individual is required – objectivity is necessary. In *King Lear* Shakespeare constructed a tragedy built round the same values and social critique as *Hamlet* but he made the meaning visible through the action.

The primitive character of the dramaturgy of *Hamlet*, discussed in regard to the fishmonger scene, becomes clearer if the play is compared with *King Lear*. Two passages that are in many respects analogous – Hamlet's 'I know not seems' speech (I.ii) and Cordelia's 'nothing' interchange (I.i) – provide a good basis for comparison. In both, the protagonists assert their integrity against a court that places more value on image than truth.

Hamlet's resistance of the Court has the attractiveness of adolescent insistence on truth. It is possible, however, that an audience may be charmed by his integrity and accept in principle that true being is preferable to 'seeming' without locating his criticism in any specific practice; i.e., attention can remain focused on the psyche of the hero – his posture of adolescent rebellion – and nodding agreement can be given to his critique without any recognition of the fundamental conflict between the attitudes of Hamlet and the Court. Since Claudius speaks reasonably (in fact he tells Laertes, 'You cannot speak of reason to the Dane/ And lose your voice' – LL.44–5), his position can appear as valid as Hamlet's; Hamlet's critique need not be accepted. Whether the Court is excused or judged corrupt, Shakespeare does not control the perspective in which events are seen by the audience. The material for judgement is presented but the case is not made.

Cordelia's 'nothing' passage, although it may seem to have a similar construction, is tightly controlled. On the basis of a bald summary of the events isolated from their dramatic embodiment – two sisters fulfil the demands of the love test, the third refuses the conditions – one might judge Cordelia to be proud and self-righteous, ruining her father's retirement ceremony on the

basis of an adolescent insistence on pure truth. But the concreteness of the play does not permit the variety of perspectives
available to abstraction; the audience is orientated by the drama
to accept Cordelia as right. The structure of the scene is similar to
that of Hamlet – and in logic she could be wrong – but the
experience of the play does not accommodate doubts about
Cordelia's rightness or her father's error.

Both the scenes have a context of ceremony and formality, and
both characters disrupt the occasion. But *King Lear*, unlike
Hamlet, has prepared the audience to recognise an alternative to a
face-value reading of the scene. In the initial exchange between
Kent and Gloucester the ceremony is viewed from outside by
those who are organising it, like Brechtian stagehands, allowing
the audience to see it as a construction. The ceremony is a special
occasion, distinct from everyday reality. And it is something
made, not natural, which means that the result is not inescapable
Fate and that it could have been made differently. This recognition of other possibilities – equivalent to questioning the reality
– is not a reasoned argument, followed logically by an audience,
but part of an atmosphere.

Both Hamlet and Cordelia destabilise the ceremonial situation
with contrary remarks. Hamlet's interventions are structurally
equivalent to asides – e.g., 'A little more than kin, and less than
kind' (I.ii.65) – but because they are personal, not connected
obviously with anything else, the audience can, like the Court,
effectively ignore them. Cordelia makes two asides before Lear
puts her to the love test:

What shall Cordelia speak? Love, and be silent.

and

    Then poor Cordelia!
And yet not so; since I am sure my love's
More ponderous than my tongue. (I.i.61,75–7)

These both undermine the rhetorical professions of love made by
her sisters, while clearly affirming her own love. She is shown not
to feel alienated from Lear or essentially at odds with the Court
(as opposed to the position Edmund reveals in soliloquy at the
beginning of the next scene), and thus she utters her 'nothing'

from positive motives. The possibility of there being a critical posture that is positive and the fact that Cordelia loves Lear are established *before* she lets drop her 'nothing' bombshell.

The preparatory manoeuvres to Cordelia's remarks may have no more effect than allowing the audience to entertain the possible validity of her position, without going so far as to establish her as being right. The subsequent behaviour of other characters does, however, validate her position. Kent is explicit in regard to Cordelia's love ('Thy youngest daughter does not love thee least' – l.151), and insists on asserting it in the face of Lear's hostility, for which he is banished. Although Burgundy in turn rejects Cordelia when she has lost royal favour and her dowry, France is eloquent about her virtues and takes her, dowerless, as his queen. And finally her sisters, no friends to her, regard Lear's rejection of her as madness: 'with what poor judgment he hath now cast her off appears too grossly' (ll. 289–91), Goneril says. The playworld thus seconds Cordelia's judgement.

Hamlet, on the other hand, is marginalised through the Court's perceiving him as mad, and thus the playworld gives little guidance to the audience in judging his responses. (In Grigori Kozintsev's film the characterisation of the Court does in fact provide guidance for the audience, but this is created through the choice of focus and sequence of images – e.g., close-ups of hard, stuffy expressions on the faces of the courtiers – which are means beyond the possibilities of conventional staging.) The *Lear* playworld has been made to confirm Cordelia's responses. Cordelia is not more right than Hamlet, but Shakespeare has organised for her a dramatic structure of support which was missing for Hamlet.

The objectivity achieved in *King Lear* can be broken down into objectivity in Shakespeare's analysis and emphasis of objectivity in his presentation. In practice they are not really separable but, for purposes of discussion, I will treat them separately and then look at the relation between objectivity and tragic form.

One of the areas of greatest objectification in *King Lear* is the development of a sense of a system that dominates the playworld. This is one of the things Lear learns for the audience. Behaviour that he at first understood as separate hostile acts – Goneril

slighting him, Regan stocking Kent, the sisters supporting each
other in denying his wishes – is by the end of Act II seen by Lear
as a coherent *pattern*. If the audience is slower than the old King,
by the time Edmund's self-interest tolerates the blinding of
Gloucester, they can hardly fail to recognise that this behaviour is
systematic. It is systematic in the sense that principles, per-
ceptions and values are interconnected and shared by the characters; the pattern of their behaviour results from a common
understanding of the world and view of the proper place of
humanity in it. The pattern which Lear comes finally to grasp
does not depend on his consciousness; it exists independently in
the playworld for the audience to see. Lear's dramatic function is
to lead the audience to it, to make them conscious of what is
shown to be already part of the playworld.

The simplest aspect of *King Lear's* systematic quality is the
development of characters into types, characters integrated into
the plot on the basis of a defined social perspective rather than on
the basis of purely personal characteristics. At one level this
amounts to little more than distinguishing qualities that were
earlier present without specific articulation. For example, in *King
Lear* Oswald's behaviour is the enactment of certain social
attitudes, whereas his likely prototypes, Osric or Rosencrantz and
Guildenstern in *Hamlet*, have a behaviour that is similar but
which is less defined as part of a complex of attitudes – it is not
made clear how their behaviour stems from social outlook.
Similarly, in Polonius's behaviour there may be recognised
significant aspects of the late sixteenth century but these seem
independent of his typicality, which is based on dramatic function (the senex) more than social attitudes.

The development of type can be seen clearly in Shakespeare's
use of the characteristic of age. Old people appear frequently in
the plays, and the way they are used evolves from dramatic
function to a social typicality that can be recognised from the
world of the audience. Thus Vincentio, father of Lucentio, in *The
Taming of the Shrew* is no more than the dramatic senex, Aegeon
in *The Comedy of Errors* little more. Old age in 1 *Henry VI* is
linked to rich memory, as with Edmund Mortimer, but has little
significance in itself. However, in *Richard II*, *Henry IV* and *Henry
V* age begins to be related to different characteristics of social

order. The dying John of Gaunt castigates the young King Richard for fracturing the old harmony and unity. Shallow and Silence are in touch with 'the good old days', times very different from the turmoil and corruption of the present. Henry V encourages his troops before the battle of Agincourt with a vision of the future offered up in terms of the past. The men are given a vision of how their victory will enter popular consciousness, even to the honour they will receive when they are old. The picture is drawn, not from the present world the audience knows, but from an imagined harmonious past – old age is associated with old times. Hamlet treats old age in a-similar way, picturing his father as old and bathed in the light of a concord that is inaccessible to the corruption and military mobilisation of the present. In *All's Well that Ends Well* the old Countess of Rossillion provides a contrast of old-style values to the self-centred behaviour of the up-to-date Court.

Shakespeare's old men become more complex through development, not only of their personal character but of their social role. And this is at the same time a transition from dramatic function – how the role fits into the play as a play – to something that is also a social function, a role recognisable as typical in the playworld. Thus in *King Lear* the old men, though not completely associated with the good, represent certain positive aspects of society which are disappearing in the present. Lear, Gloucester, Kent, Albany, the old tenant all display some shared sense of a social world into which they are integrated, a sense clearly absent among the youthful representatives of individualism.

The values of the types are tested by practice. This allows for contradictory behaviour and mixed judgements and gives a naturalistic credibility to characters that might otherwise seem simplistic. Thus Gloucester's bluff good nature, for example, which has a positive role in supporting social integrity and helping Lear, is at the same time coupled with an insensitivity that encourages him to proceed by habit rather than from observation of what happens in front of him. This is not particularly blameworthy in itself, except insofar as self-indulgence fosters the generation of self-interested Edmund types. Cause and effect become very complicated when seen as part of the interconnectedness of phenomena.

As well as serving an analytic function, the use of types has considerable advantages for presentation. The clarity of social analysis in *Lear* is in fact part of the *aesthetic* effect. The construction of types produces a group of characteristics that are, as it were, 'pre-evaluated'; the significance is supplied with the type, facilitating the argument. Attention is selective; we cannot take in all the features of a scene at a single moment. Where types are recognised in a scene, much is already known without requiring directed thinking on the part of the audience – they are free to attend to what is novel in the scene. For example, when Goneril confronts Lear in Act I, scene iv, having decided in the previous scene to restrict his freedom, an audience can understand it as an action motivated by a rational individualism, the defining characteristic of one of the play's main types. Thus they can attend to the conflict that results, without being distracted by the search for a motive for the behaviour – Goneril behaves that way because that is the kind of person, the type, she is. Similarly, the conflict between Lear and his daughters that culminates in his 'reason not the need' speech (Act II, scene iv) is more than just a hostile encounter of personalities whose motivations must be understood in all their diversity. It is clearer, sharper and more intense because the confrontation is between two definitions of humanity, two types, that come already loaded with emotional attitude, more than can be generated in the scene from previously undefined behaviour. Thus an otherwise minor interchange that breaks the convention can produce an enormously magnified effect on playworld and audience. Cordelia's simple 'nothing' in Lear's love test, because it focuses a conflict between the complexes of attitudes found in types, produces enormous reverberations. Because type generalises (rather than negates) personal experience, it can also lead an audience to see the relevance of the issues to themselves, part of the mirror that Hamlet says theatre holds up to nature.

Shakespeare's objectification through type is artistically very efficient. The growing hostility between Goneril and Albany, the transfer of her affections to Edmund and the alienation of her husband, is plot material that, as well as part of a sequence of events, is made typical, a parallel instance of the other conflicts. The scene opens with an indication of Goneril's personal antagonism for her husband and her view that his unassertive manner demonstrates cowardly lack of spirit – 'he'll not feel wrongs/ Which tie him to an answer' (IV.ii.13–14). Albany rejects her, but in a way that expresses the personal response within a systematic moral view. The personal encounter partakes of the typical, without being any less personal:

> That nature, which contemns it origin,
> Cannot be border'd certain in itself;
> She that herself will sliver and disbranch
> From her material sap, perforce must wither
> And come to deadly use. (IV.ii.32–6)

Albany's argument then turns to an application of the systematic view to the particular offence – calling for a punishment that we know has already taken place.

> What have you done?
> Tigers, not daughters, what have you perform'd?
> A father, and a gracious aged man,
> Whose reverence even the head-lugg'd bear would lick,
> Most barbarous, most degenerate! have you madded.
> Could my good brother suffer you to do it?
> A man, a prince, by him so benefited!
> If that the heavens do not their visible spirits
> Send quickly down to tame these vilde offences,
> It will come,
> Humanity must perforce prey on itself,
> Like monsters of the deep. (IV.ii.39–50)

Goneril counters Albany with an attack that integrates the personal and typical. It is intended to injure but also expresses a different set of moral criteria – personal benefit:

> Milk-liver'd man!
> That bear'st a cheek for blows, a head for wrongs;
> Who hast not in thy brows an eye discerning
> Thine honour from thy suffering; that not know'st
> Fools do those villains pity who are punish'd
> Ere they have done their mischief. (IV.ii.50–5)

Into what is now a focusing of opposition of systems comes a messenger to Albany with news of Cornwall's death, who says matter-of-factly that he was slain while 'going to put out/ The

other eye of Gloucester' (IV.ii.71–2). The event itself was earlier
presented, most unusually on-stage, in all its horror. The idea of
retribution has already been introduced by Albany; the blinding
of Gloucester and the death of Cornwall confirm his system and
suggest the quality of prophesy fulfilled:

> This shows you are above,
> You justicers, that these our nether crimes
> So speedily can venge! (IV.ii.78–80)

For the audience the rehearsing of an event already witnessed
makes it at once seem less unusual and, because it could be
reported so calmly, more monstrous. The clash of two systems
reverberates with a force that far exceeds the potential of isolated
events.

The horror of the event is increased by Albany's looking for
exceptions, for an innocent party: he asks if Edmund knows of
the wickedness. The messenger says:

> Ay, my good Lord; 'twas he inform'd against him,
> And quit the house on purpose that their punishment
> Might have the freer course. (IV.ii.92–4)

Casual events can be avoided; a system seems inescapable. The
focusing power of this interchange is to transform the cinematic
immediacy of blood-and-guts horror to something that is characteristic of one system of behaviour. Shakespeare leaves no space
for comment. The messenger answers Albany's question about
Gloucester's other eye and, without interruption, turns to his
business with Goneril. The meaning has been made to exist
objectively in the events – no comment is necessary.

The character of Lear himself is part of Shakespeare's presenta-
tional skill in achieving objectivity. In *Hamlet*, apart from
structural obstacles to objectivity, there is an encouragement to
subjectivity in the character of the hero. The attractiveness of
Hamlet makes audiences *want* to accept his judgements and to
see things through his eyes. Hamlet does not have to be right for
us to take his point of view; but because we are willing to see
things his way on the basis of affection, what we agree to seems
to be less important – it is arrived at by a process of personal
identification that had nothing to do with what was judged ('I'll

believe anything he tells me!'). Lear, on the other hand, is a tiresome old man who does not attract audience affection. Pity, yes, but not affection. He is also a hero of singularly bad judgement, as is pointed out both to him and the audience, which further discourages unexamined acceptance of his views. Contrary to our relation to Hamlet, we are placed in a position of observing Lear rather than identifying with him. What we learn is how he misunderstands, what he comes to understand and feel. We are then in a position to view events objectively but, because we have witnessed the process of their shattering effect on Lear, feelingly as well. Objectification is aesthetic as well as rational. The unity of understanding and emotion has been made possible by Shakespeare's combining the personal and typical, by his objectification of the tragedy.

Decentring the tragedy

The objectification of *King Lear* makes the significance of events more comprehensible and, with the reduced prominence of personal perspectives that accompanies the process, it also changes the nature of the tragedy. The traditional view, deriving ultimately from distortions of Aristotle, makes the process of tragedy an individual experience. The hero falls as a result of a 'tragic flaw' and the tragedy is seen to reside in that individual destruction. Almost all of Shakespeare's tragedy can be pressed into this mould, but results in simplistic renderings, such as 'Macbeth falls because he is ambitious', 'Othello falls because he is jealous', etc. Hamlet is subject to a larger range of possibilities, but the result is still that effect and cause are located in the hero.

This model of tragedy does not work for *King Lear*. Whereas Macbeth, the witches notwithstanding, might be said himself to generate the conditions that bring about his downfall, as well as himself committing the fatal act, for Lear the conditions are shown to be something over which he has no control. He does no more than precipitate a catastrophe where things were already about to fall. An argument for Lear as the principal cause could more reasonably be entertained if the play ended with Act III. In that case Lear, even if not convincingly the cause of the tragedy, would be certainly its subject, the character whose history makes up the plot. In the last ten scenes, however, the action moves away from Lear, decentring the tragedy from the individual.

When Kent enters in Act V, scene iii, and inquires of the King, 'Is he not here?', Albany replies, 'Great thing of us forgot!' (V.iii.235). This characterises the decentring of the tragedy. How can it be Lear's tragedy when for a significant portion of the play Lear in effect disappears, for both the other characters and the audience? If the hero is forgotten, then it is not his tragedy. In *King Lear* the focus is purposefully dislocated from the hero to the world in which he moves; it is the tragedy, not of an individual, but of a society.

In the second half of the play, where the tragedy is decentred from Lear, we see the breaking of Gloucester, the death of Cornwall, Goneril and Regan coming into conflict and their destruction. The effect of this is an aspect of objectification – we feel the tragedy through Lear but it is not just his tragedy. The tragic action is perceived as part of a larger process, as part of a system. The final destruction of Cordelia and Lear is presented not as the culmination of a personal history but as another part, the end, of a social upheaval. The tragedy is inescapably social.

Lear is a victim, not because of anything personally special, but because he is caught in a movement not of his own making, on a scale almost beyond his comprehension. 'Men make their own history,' said Marx, 'but they do not make it just as they please' (Marx, K., and Engels, F. (1979), *The Eighteenth Brumaire of Louis Bonaparte*; Collected Works, Vol II, Lawrence and Wishart, London, p. 103).

The questions that arise in regard to the peculiarity of having a tragic hero experience two downfalls are inappropriate; Lear's second victimisation is almost random – he is 'food for powder' rather than a chosen victim – as his own words of pain and incomprehension suggest: 'Why should a dog, a horse, a rat, have life,/ And thou no breath at all?' (V.iii.305–6). He is a victim without there being a reason. It is the process of the system – the subject of the tragedy is the society.

In *King Lear* the conflict that troubled Shakespeare from the Second History Cycle through the tragedies is objectified, and the experience of the play even for today's audiences is shattering. Whether or not one chooses to regard it as the high point of

Shakespeare's dramatic development, its intensity of feeling is related to the clarity of its vision. And that clarity provided the basis for the tragedies that followed.

Macbeth begins where *King Lear* finishes. The positive aspect of the end of *Lear* – that the King is at last clear about what is important – does not change the pessimistic reality, and the reign of King Edgar does not look promising. Systematic problems are not resolved by the deaths of individuals. In *Macbeth* Shakespeare uses the understanding of *King Lear* and begins to examine the tragic conditions again, in terms of the individual. He explores the personal manifestations of the breakdown of social order in a tragedy that, though it gains its depth and significance from its social resonance, is constructed through the motivations and experience of an individual.

CHAPTER V

Macbeth

Shakespeare could dramatise the intensity of psychological conflict in *Macbeth* only because he had already made clear the terms.
In *King Lear* he showed through events what individualism
meant for society, in *Macbeth* what it meant for the individual.
The massive conflicts of the Lear world, objectified and defined,
are compressed in *Macbeth* into the consciousness of a single
person.

In one sense this makes *Macbeth* Shakespeare's most taut, most
efficient and most classical tragedy, yet it has acquired a reputation as a very difficult play to stage well. This may have
something to do with its exceptional degree of spectacle and with
genuine staging problems – such as the darkness and semi-
darkness of much of the play, the amount of violence and the
number of fights, and the materiality/immateriality of the witches
and Banquo's ghost. It may also owe something to the way that,
perhaps more than any other Shakespeare play, *Macbeth* has been
treated as literature. Its consistent imagery, polish, symbolic
scenes, etc. have made it particularly susceptible to literary study.
Furthermore, the extra-theatrical influences to which the creation
of the play was subject – e.g., the supposed need for Shakespeare
to flatter King James and appeal to his interest in witchcraft,
Scotland and the divine quality of kings – would seem even
today to place a considerable strain on production.

The variety of material and concerns found in *Macbeth* has
generated a range of seemingly different plays, such as studies of
evil, statements on the uncertainty of rule, a balletic examination
of the interaction of inner force with external powers. A surpris-
ing number of these interpretations – from the subtle psychological reading to the crude blood-and-thunder action narrative

– are viable. Looking at the play as a metaphor for social disintegration, I believe, can make sense of it as a whole, can help explain its peculiar stylistic variations, and integrate its diversity in a unified intention.

It may at first seem strange to speak of *Macbeth* as picturing further deterioration of the world of *King Lear* when that play is so apocalyptic in character. *Macbeth* could scarcely contain more suffering and violence, and Macbeth's ambition is no worse than Edmund's. The element of decline is seen not in a continuation or an intensification of the clash between social and individualistic behaviour but, paradoxically, in a confusion of the two. Although in *Lear* individualistic attitudes are initially given some approval, the positive and negative aspects are sharply differentiated. In *Macbeth* the distinctions are not so clear. Macbeth's individualistic attitude is at one with his military heroics, a part of his social virtue, recognised as such by the playworld and probably by the audience as well. In *Lear* Shakespeare showed what individualism was, what its consequences were, but *Macbeth* is organised to explore the reasons why someone would choose to behave in that way. Because audiences raised on psychological novels probably find this approach more interesting than the charting of a social landscape, it may seem both natural and a technical advance on Shakespeare's part, but it also indicates that the play has a lower estimate of the consciousness of the contemporary audience. That is, in *Lear* the argument depends only on showing the evidence – the action makes the point ('you can see what happens when . . .' etc.) – whereas in *Macbeth* Shakespeare must interpret the evidence and has to show *why* it is bad. This suggests that Shakespeare is addressing an audience with a greater tolerance for individualistic behaviour, more habituated to it.

Social disintegration in *Macbeth* may be less immediately recognisable because the play returns to the complication of *Hamlet* and the events of the plot are again a *vehicle* for constructing an argument (as opposed to *King Lear*, where the plot presents what the play is about). Even more than with *Hamlet*, *Macbeth*'s plot has been accepted as the theme of the play. Whereas Hamlet's inaction somewhat decentres the revenge plot, the crime-and-retribution framework for events in *Macbeth* can attract audience attention to the mere working out of the narrative. The tragedy then may be reduced to the story of a bad man who commits a crime in order to become King and is punished by being overthrown and killed, a play of mere action.

But the primary difficulty of *Macbeth* is its slipperiness. Not only do circumstances change but the terms used to define them shift in their meaning, which is often distinguished as the play's reliance on paradox. *Macbeth* is concerned with means and ends, and though these may appear to have an obvious relationship, the consequences of realised actions are often disastrously different from their anticipated significance.

Macbeth's internalisation of the conflict between individual-istic and socialised behaviour necessarily makes the play more complicated than *King Lear*. This is in part because the play includes more material – the relations depicted in *King Lear* as well as processes of individual psychology – but also because Macbeth cannot be pigeon-holed: he is both good and bad, social and individualistic, in behaviour and feeling. As a warrior he is heroic and is socialised in serving the welfare of his nation, but as a regicide he is the reverse. In his pursuit of kingship he is viciously ambitious, but in his doubts and the agonies of his remorse, he assumes a clearly social attitude.

Macbeth is not critically heroic, like Cordelia, nor does he withstand public opinion, like Hamlet; he follows the social code. He is shallow, unsure in his own position, unclear in any precise way about what he wants – but he wants what is socially approved. He reflects the environment, is moulded by it without altering the mould. Like qualities that are transformed into their opposites yet remain the same, like the ambition that 'o'erleaps itself and falls on th'other' (I.vii.27–8), his vices are only different aspects of his virtue. Through this weak, impressionable consciousness, Shakespeare explores the values of the world in which he moves.

Abstractions cannot explain this process, for the terms acquire meaning only in context and the meanings shift with changing contexts. The second scene opens with the report of bloody battle, destruction and treason. Because it is in the service of the King – maintaining the state against rebellion and foreign invasion – the context bestows approval. The latent contra-diction between praise and gore is deferred by the rhetorical character of the language, which distances the slaughter. Macbeth's ambition is seen at this stage not as something bad in itself, but as a necessary concomitant of his military virtue, more neutral than Caesar's ambition. It is not a quality distinguished from other traits and isolated in a villain but something present as part of the virtue of the hero.

Macbeth and social context

The complexity of Macbeth's social context is most clearly objectified in the banquet scene (III.iv). Almost immediately Macbeth has achieved the kingship – 'He is already nam'd, and gone to Scone/ To be invested' (II.iv.31–2) – the banquet is mentioned. In the scene that follows, Macbeth and Lady Macbeth respectively greet Banquo with 'Here's our chief guest' and 'If he had been forgotten,/ It had been as a gap in our great feast' (III.i.11–12). The banquet scene is thus the *dramatic* confirmation of kingship, of special importance given the audience's knowledge that Macbeth is a murderer and given Banquo's doubts, articulated immediately before he is cast as 'chief guest':

> Thou hast it now, King, Cawdor, Glamis, all,
> As the Weïrd Women promis'd; and, I fear,
> Thou play'dst most foully for't. (III.i.1–3)

The occasion is ceremonial – the confirmation of Macbeth's kingship specifically and, generally, of social integrity, of community. The shared consumption of food is, at the most fundamental level, the assertion of consubstantiality – having partaken of the same substance, they *are* all the same substance. They are breaking bread together, like religious communicants becoming part of the body of Christ through eating the wafer/ body and drinking the wine/blood of Christ. It is of course not just technical consubstantiality that is the end of the banquet, but spiritual togetherness (also like communion) – as Lady Macbeth herself says, uttering sentiments that are appropriate even if they do not reflect her own outlook:

> You do not give the cheer: the feast is sold,
> That is not often vouch'd, while 'tis a-making,
> 'Tis given with welcome: to feed were best at home;

From thence, the sauce to meat is ceremony;
Meeting were bare without it. (III.iv.32–6)

If the feast functions properly, Macbeth becomes part of, head of,
a unified body politic.

But Macbeth is barred literally and symbolically from the feast.
Rosse invites him to sit, but Macbeth is unable to find a free place
and says simply 'The table's full'. Lenox then says to the king,
'Here is a place reserv'd, Sir', and when Macbeth still does not see
it, he repeats, 'Here, my good Lord' (III.iv.45,47). At that point
Macbeth sees that it is the ghost of Banquo that fills up his place.
This is an emblem, a concretisation of Macbeth's social relations:
his deeds, the murder of Banquo, bar him from joining the
community. Literally and metaphorically, there is no place for
him.

The order of community still remains – Macbeth relies on the
lords knowing their own degrees to seat themselves at the
banquet and Lady Macbeth, to speed their departure, must voice
the demand that they dispense with such order:

Stand not upon the order of your going,
But go at once. (III.iv.118–19)

Even if he violates it himself, Macbeth assumes an order that
comes from community:

Blood hath been shed ere now, i'th'olden time,
Ere humane statute purg'd the gentle weal;
. . .
    the time has been,
That, when the brains were out, the man would die,
And there an end; but now, they rise again,
With twenty mortal murthers on their crowns,
And push us from our stools. (III.iv.74–81)

Ghosts are in some way primitive and uncivilised; proper social
order would keep Banquo dead. Macbeth has alienated himself
from the community in which he was to realise his ambition.

The appearance of the ghost is not casual – dramatically it is
juxtaposed with the murder of Banquo (it is the scene that
follows) and the murderers themselves briefly intrude at the

banquet. The ghost arrives in response to Macbeth's utterance –
Macbeth says:

> Here had we now our country's honour roof'd,
> Were the grac'd person of our Banquo present.
>   (III.iv.39–40)

And the ghost enters. Its second entry is preceded by another call
for Banquo:

> I drink to th'general joy o'th'whole table,
> And to our dear friend Banquo, whom we miss;
> Would he were here! (III.iv.88–90)

Banquo's presence is needed to complete the social integrity –
'our country's honour roof'd'; the ghost, an image, mocks the
'country's honour', reduced to only an image by Macbeth.

At one remove, the disruption of the banquet symbolises
Macbeth's guilt – his sins return to haunt him, his deeds exclude
him from the social whole. This has the literal, objectified side
represented by his finding there is no place for him at the table,
but it has also the internalised side of *feeling* guilty – Macbeth is
experiencing the deep remorse that goes beyond the technical
recognition of having committed a crime. Unlike Claudius, who
shows no signs of guilt until he is upset at the 'mousetrap' and
whose prayers in the next scene still suggest a sense of formal
guilt rather than remorse ('May one be pardon'd and retain
th'offence?' – III.iii.56), Macbeth worries less about retribution
than about recognising himself to be the kind of person he does
not want to be. His guilt is part of the same sentiment that speaks
against killing Duncan in the first place and almost stops him. It is
a question of how humanity or being a man is defined, of how he
would define himself.

Definitions of humanity

Macbeth has sought honour, the good regard of the population,
and he has won it through heroic conduct in defence of Scotland.
He could avoid the contradiction between seeking highest
honour and personal treachery by remaining as he is, honoured
but not king:

We will proceed no further in this business:
He hath honour'd me of late; and I have bought
Golden opinions from all sorts of people,
Which would be worn now in their newest gloss,
Not cast aside so soon. (I.vii.31–5)

Lady Macbeth reproaches him for cowardice, for being unwilling
to take what he wants, for as she said of him earlier, he is
unwilling 'to catch the nearest way' (I.v.18) because he is 'too full
o'th'milk of human kindness' (I.v.17), affected by a sense of
kinship with others of his kind. Her logic has the same rational
clarity as Edmund's, posed as a question that allows only one
answer:

Would'st thou have that
Which thou esteem'st the ornament of life,
And live a coward in thine own esteem? (I.vii.41–3)

But Macbeth's reply proposes a different definition of humanity:

I dare do all that may become a man;
Who dares do more, is none. (I.vii.46–7)

His definition is social, a fitting into rather than an exceeding.
Lady Macbeth counters with a definition of Man that is individualistic, where Man implies dominance instead of co-
operation:

When you durst do it, then you were a man;
And, to be more than what you were, you would
Be so much more the man . . . (I.vii.49–51)

Ruthless pursuit of desire, as with Edmund, constitutes Man for
Lady Macbeth. Her Man is an exaggeration of certain human
qualities, like some of the grotesques produced by body-building
– the winner is the Man – whereas for Macbeth, Man is defined
by a relation to the rest of humanity, is a Man by virtue of
qualities that exist only in the sharing. Manliness for him is not an
absolute quality such that the more it is present, the more manly
is the man; rather, it involves a balance of qualities which can be
destroyed by excess. Lady Macbeth takes an atomistic view of
society and thus defines humanity in terms of the biological
creature – the 'bare, forked animal' recognised by Lear

(III.iv.106) – which depends only on what is present in the single individual; someone growing up alone on a desert island is for her as much Man potentially as someone raised in civil society.

In the same way that Shakespeare emphasises and clarifies conduct in *King Lear* by repeating it in parallel relationships (the double plot), in *Macbeth* he repeats this confrontation over definitions of man in Act IV, scene iii, where Macduff learns of the murder of his family. When Rosse finally delivers the terrible news, Macduff starts to crumble (indicated by Malcolm's 'What, man! ne'er pull your hat upon your brows' – IV.iii.208). Malcolm reassures him, offering an eye for an eye as the 'cure' for Macduff's own loss:

> Be comforted:
> Let's make us med'cines of our great revenge,
> To cure this deadly grief. (IV.iii.213–15)

His position is encapsulated in his saying to Macduff, 'Dispute it like a man' (IV.iii.220), Macduff's by his reply, 'But I must also feel it as a man' (IV.iii.221). Macduff is using a definition of 'man' that reproduces the sense of a social being expressed by Macbeth – an emotional relationship with others is part of being Man – while Malcolm's restricted focus on violent behaviour echoes the machismo of Lady Macbeth.

Lady Macbeth's husband yields to the hardness of her reasoning – 'If we should fail?' (I.vii.59), he says, giving hypothetical acceptance to the murder. He accepts the logical connection between his desired end and the means, but he still has doubts. The dilemma is that if he acts, then he denies his principles, and if he does not act, then he denies his desires. His goal is kingship, yet he cannot escape the reverberations of his deed, cannot 'jump the life to come' or escape from 'this bank and shoal of time' (I.vii.7,6). The conflict, between narrow expediency and social principle, can find no resolution.

The seeming ease with which Macbeth can abandon his definition of mankind to follow Lady Macbeth is partly explained by his desire for kingship, but it also occurs because he *is* weak – he 'wouldst not play false,/ And yet wouldst wrongly win' (I.v.21–2). He can be courageous in doing what is expected of

him but he is weak in making up his mind; his initial resistance to
Lady Macbeth's plan is on the basis of a principle not his own.

This weakness is seen in the first moral challenge he is
presented with – his response to the witches. Macbeth's social
thinking is not an articulated, coherent set of principles, which
makes him less able to tolerate contemplating antisocial behaviour; i.e., merely to think something antisocial is for Macbeth to
be guilty of wishing it into being, for he calls it into being in
thought. This explains the severity of the disturbance he
experiences when the witches greet him with 'All hail, Macbeth!
that shalt be King hereafter' (I.iii.50). Shakespeare makes a point
of the disturbance, objectifies it, by having Banquo say to
Macbeth:

> Good Sir, why do you start, and seem to fear
> Things that do sound so fair? (I.iii.51–2)

Banquo also says to the witches that Macbeth 'seems rapt withal'
(I.iii.57) but, in contrast, is himself able to ask with equanimity
about his own future. When Rosse and Angus greet Macbeth as
Cawdor, an earnest of the witches' prophecy, Macbeth is again
'rapt', as Banquo makes explicit (I.iii.143), and which Macbeth
acknowledges by apologising for it (I.iii.150–1). Shakespeare
underscores it again in having Macbeth refuse to face his
disturbance, twice approaching it indirectly, distancing himself
from it by changing the focus to Banquo by saying to him, 'Your
children shall be kings' (I.iii.86).

The point here is not wicked disguise of motive (as in *Richard
III*) nor is it jealous worry about Banquo's intrusion in the
succession; it is childlike inability to entertain a thought he must
regard as disloyal, the guilty dream. Loyalty is not for Macbeth
the complex of diverse habits, principles and impulses that it is
for, say, Enobarbus in *Antony and Cleopatra*; it is conventional
and simplistic:

> The service and the loyalty I owe,
> In doing it, pays itself. Your Highness' part
> Is to receive our duties: and our duties
> Are to your throne and state, children and servants;
> Which do but what they should, by doing everything
> Safe toward your love and honour. (I.iv.22–7)

This conventional statement does not reflect Macbeth's view, even if it does not conceal a contrary position (he is no Edmund); he is following the fashion. When the witches prophesy his kingship he is too weak to risk the integrity of his view of loyalty by considering a contrary notion. He can cite conclusions (as on loyalty) but cannot cope with contradictions.

The 'murther' that is yet but 'fantastical' is not the plot to dispose of Duncan (Macbeth is not like Claudius) but embarrassed recognition that for him to be king, Duncan must be dead. That is, for Macbeth to think of himself as king, he must remove Duncan in thought, willingly, which is sufficient for embarrassment, both tactless and disloyal. This is given dramatic contrast with Banquo's equilibrium. Banquo is not lacking in interest in advancement, as his comment on Duncan's dispensing of rewards indicates. When Duncan tells Macbeth, now elevated to Thane of Cawdor, 'I have begun to plant thee, and will labour/ To make thee full of growing', and then tells Banquo who 'hast no less deserv'd', 'let me infold thee,/ And hold thee in my heart', Banquo makes a witty rejoinder: 'There if I grow,/ The harvest is your own' (I.iv.28–33). Banquo can entertain the prophecies of the witches, can feel ambition, without embarrassment; thinking is not guilty for him. His principles are his own and he can therefore deal with contradictions.

In the action-story reading of the play, Macbeth's saying 'My thought, whose murther yet is but fantastical' (I.iii.139) is often taken to indicate that he started to contemplate murdering Duncan as soon as he heard the witches' words or even earlier. There is nothing else in the play that suggests this and it is quite unnecessary. Duncan is old, Macbeth is the likely successor and his blood-shedding has been limited to socially commendable situations. Macbeth first thinks murderous (as opposed to social slaying) thoughts when, immediately after the dispensing of rewards and Banquo's sarcastic reply, the king announces Malcolm as successor to the throne:

> Sons, kinsmen, Thanes,
> And you whose places are the nearest, know,
> We will establish our estate upon
> Our eldest, Malcolm; whom we name hereafter
> The Prince of Cumberland: (I.iv.35–9)

Here Macbeth's response is calculating:

> That is a step
> On which I must fall down, or else o'erleap,
> For in my way it lies.

And it is also consciously murderous:

> Stars, hide your fires!
> Let not light see my black and deep desires;
> The eye wink at the hand; yet let that be,
> Which the eye fears, when it is done, to see. (I.iv.48–53)

When he is 'rapt' at the witches' truth, his thought is of a very different character, emotional rather than calculating.

The problem of Macbeth's emotional weakness, his inability to face his desires as well as his deeds, is continued throughout the play. Even when he is established in his murderous career, when he can say, after the murder of Banquo, 'I am in blood/ Stepp'd in so far, that, should I wade no more,/ Returning were as tedious as go o'er' (III.iv.135–7), he is still unable to adjust his criteria of behaviour to fit the deeds he is now habituated to. He announces to Lady Macbeth when he has commissioned the murder of Banquo, 'there shall be done/ A deed of dreadful note' (III.ii.43–4), but cannot face it directly when she inquires what it is:

> Be innocent of the knowledge, dearest chuck,
> Till thou applaud the deed. Come, seeling Night,
> Scarf up the tender eye of pitiful Day,
> And, with thy bloody and invisible hand,
> Cancel, and tear to pieces, that great bond
> Which keeps me pale! (III.ii.45–50)

This is equivalent to his addressing the 'sure and firm-set earth' in Act II, scene i, as he readies himself to murder Duncan:

> Hear not my steps, which way they walk, for fear
> Thy very stones prate of my where-about,
> And take the present horror from the time,
> Which now suits with it. (II.i.57–60)

Macbeth here recognises a fundamental contradiction between his action and what he would regard as his nature. To kill Duncan, he asks for what is effectively a suspension of nature, during which time he can perform his terrible deed. In order to kill Banquo, he intensifies his demand: not only a darkness which, like suspended nature, will keep his deed from sight (including his own), but also a cancellation of what he sees as his relation to the rest of humanity, his social bond. Only by severing himself from collective humanity, the sense of Man he earlier opposed to Lady Macbeth's ideal of unlimited will, can he commit the antisocial outrage he contemplates. He goes beyond suspension of his nature; he must now, in cancelling the social bond, deny it.

The terms Macbeth uses here to speak of 'social bond' invest the scene with contradictory overtones. The image evoked by 'bond' in the speech is that of contract, something that can be physically cancelled and, like paper or parchment, torn to pieces. It is equivalent to John of Gaunt's 'inky blots and rotten parchment bonds' which are part of his accusation of Richard, that he has become 'Landlord of England', not King (II.i.64,113). But the actual relation Macbeth is talking about here is social; the 'bond' is the social bond, the same thing according to which Cordelia loved her father. This is part of the substitution of contract for custom, individual agreement for social code, that provided part of the basis for distinguishing the villains in *King Lear*. Macbeth's hypertrophied will is associated with contract, but he still feels himself part of the social bond. He cannot violate it without violating himself, his own nature. It is like the Duke of York's warning to Richard II when he is about to seize the 'royalties and rights' of Bolingbroke and violate the rights of succession:

> take from time
> His charters, and his customary rights;
> Let not to-morrow then ensue to-day:
> Be not thyself (*Richard II*, II.i.195–8)

The ante has been raised since Duncan's murder: Macbeth knows that his own humanity is what is at stake here.

Reversal

In light of the contradictions already internalised in Macbeth, the cause of his career of violence and destruction can be seen to be present in himself. The causal function of the witches is to provide encouragement and confirm a vision that is already present, though vaguely, in Macbeth's mind. For the audience, they articulate the paradoxical quality of the play – 'Fair is foul, and foul is fair'. Their primary function is theatrical: they provide a spectacular element that makes a good show, which is symbolic and produces meaning in casting its eerie pall over the scenes and events that follow. Thus Macbeth and Banquo, in effect, walk in the shadow of the witches once the prophecies have been uttered. The atmosphere generated by the witches in the first scene influences the perception of what follows. The description of Macbeth's bloody heroism, for example, is made more unsettling by the shadow lingering from the witches' 'fair is foul'. Lady Macbeth also goes through a process of reversal in her 'unsex me here' speech. It is contrary to, opposed to Nature ('That no compunctious visitings of Nature/ Shake my fell purpose' – I.v.45–6) and destabilises the order of nature.

The nature or matter of the witches has often been seen as 'Evil' and this is sometimes regarded as the subject matter of the play – which Macbeth then catches like a virus. But the witches' evil is non-specific, or rather, it is atmospheric. When Macbeth asks them, 'What is't you do?', they reply, 'A deed without a name' (IV.i.49). This is more than a statement that what they do is anonymous; their activity is so outside society it does not even have the minimal social conception of a name. Macbeth's evil, on the other hand, has a very specific manifestation in murder and destruction and has also a specific motivation – the unbridled individualism that must be covered by 'seeling night'.

In the same way that he avoids substituting abstractions for concrete behaviour, Shakespeare never allows Macbeth to be simplified into the victim of a single characteristic; motives in *Macbeth* are unfailingly presented in a social context. Ambition, once conventionally given as the characteristic responsible for Macbeth's tragic career, is not in itself dangerous or bad – it is in fact the element that makes Macbeth into the social hero described in scene ii. The problem is ambition divorced from social considerations, individualistic advantage gained outside of social processes. The complexity of motive and experience is maintained in Macbeth's own thinking, which reflects the tangled lines of causation. Thus it is never so cut and dried as recognising what is simply a wrong action, that he should not have killed Duncan after all. His deeds are important as part of a process, not just an end result.

Macbeth at one point, trying to blame the witches for his failure, gives an excellent characterisation of their duplicitous role:

> be these juggling fiends no more believ'd,
> That palter with us in a double sense;
> That keep the word of promise to our ear,
> And break it to our hope. (V.viii.19–22)

Macbeth has formulated his desires in the terms of the witches, taking what appeared to be the proper means to achieve them, but producing the wrong result, the opposite of his intention. The vision goes beyond failure; he gives a positive image of what he *should* have achieved, and there is a sense of overwhelming loss:

> I have liv'd long enough: my way of life
> Is fall'n into the sere, the yellow leaf;
> And that which should accompany old age,
> As honour, love, obedience, troops of friends,
> I must not look to have; but in their stead,
> Curses, not loud, but deep, mouth-honour, breath,
> Which the poor heart would fain deny, and dare not.
>   (V.iii.22–8)

The context gives the speech great importance – it is equivalent to Macbeth's final (actually penultimate) judgement. After his lifetime of experience, after a career of purposeful action and realisation of motives, he is at the decisive moment of his reign – 'This push/ will cheer me ever, or disseat me now' (V.iii.20–1). In the midst of extreme crisis, his life is condensed into this single judgement.

It is here that *Macbeth*'s poetry is at its richest. Its resonance is not in the conceit but in the social character of the verse. The sensual quality of the poetry, unlike the sensation of spectacle, provides a non-intellectual integration into something larger, a feeling of a language bigger than the person who uses it or the one who receives it. It is the individualist Macbeth, paradoxically, who speaks with a voice more socially resonant than that of any other of the characters, uttering speech that (as Nicholas Brooke points out[1]), goes well beyond the character himself. This emphasises, in feeling rather than logically or intellectually, the impossible contradiction lived by Macbeth, of attempting a social goal through private, antisocial means.

In saying 'I have liv'd long enough' he is saying that his life is effectively finished. He cannot hope for the rewards appropriate to his time of life, he cannot achieve the respect, fond regard and social integration that old age might hope for; he cannot achieve any of them because of what he has done. The witches have kept the letter of the promise and broken the spirit. He got what he asked for – the crown – but it did not mean what it was supposed to. For Tamburlaine kingship was an obvious goal; it was a symbol of independence and self-assertion that he and his followers wanted without questioning it. But kingship for Macbeth is more than symbolic; why he wants it, not obvious in itself, becomes clear when he articulates what it is he has lost.

The 'honour, love, obedience, troops of friends' for which Macbeth longed are instances of social affection, of which the king is the focus, the centre of the society's love, and it was there that ambition directed Macbeth. It is not a Machiavellian hankering after power or independence but the warmth of public regard. Macbeth assumed that kingship always carried with it the qualities that made it attractive to him; if he seized it the qualities should still be there. But he learned painfully what Lear learned – that kingship is a social relation, that affection comes as a result of living that relation, not as a result of occupying that space in the social pyramid.

Macbeth did not understand that the means can shape the end. The 'mouth-honour' that he receives instead of genuine respect is reminiscent of Falstaff's exposition of honour at the end of 1 *Henry IV*, mere breath. The social position cannot be achieved by individualistic means. The individualistic means may bring an appearance of the thing – something that can be called honour – but without the social resonance, the appearance is only a mockery of the real thing. And it is perhaps more painful for that,

---

[1] Introduction to The Oxford Shakespeare *Macbeth*, ed. N. Brooke (1990: Oxford University Press, Oxford), pp. 7–22.

for being and yet not being the thing it is supposed to be.
Macbeth goes beyond neutral assessment of his position and
expresses here the depths of his disappointment, his awareness
that his whole life has been a failure. He faces up to his position
that, in gaining the throne without the social resonance that is
majesty, he has only the mockery of what he wanted – that fair is
indeed foul.

He restated his evaluation of his experience immediately after the
death of Lady Macbeth, concluding that all is meaningless. He is
not being emotional, in the sense of letting emotion rather than
reason guide his speech and action; in fact his lack of response to
'the cry of women' (V.v.8) seems worthy of remark, even to him:

> I have almost forgot the taste of fears.
> The time has been, my senses would have cool'd
> To hear a night-shriek; and my fell of hair
> Would at a dismal treatise rouse, and stir,
> As life were in't. I have supp'd full with horrors:
> Direness, familiar to my slaughterous thoughts,
> Cannot once start me. (V.v.9–15)

This hardening that is the subject of his comment is deadness, not
courage. Macbeth recognises that he is finished; he has failed
definitively in his aims and now it is only a matter of awaiting the
formal conclusion; and even the meaning of that has been lost in
what has gone before, as his response to the announcement of the
Queen's death suggests: 'There would have been a time for such a
word' (V.v.18). In what is probably the best-known speech from
the play (and probably second only to *Hamlet*'s 'to be or not to
be' in its cliche status), Macbeth articulates the pointlessness of
his existence:

> To-morrow, and to-morrow, and to-morrow,
> Creeps in this petty pace from day to day,
> To the last syllable of recorded time;
> And all our yesterdays have lighted fools
> The way to dusty death. Out, out, brief candle!
> Life's but a walking shadow; a poor player,
> That struts and frets his hour upon the stage,
> And then is heard no more: it is a tale
> Told by an idiot, full of sound and fury,
> Signifying nothing. (V.v.19–28)

This is the ultimate judgement that life, not signifying anything, has no meaning.

Macbeth is not giving a Beckett-like judgement that meaning is *impossible* in life; it is his own life that has lost purpose. Meaning in life was indicated earlier in his reflection on the pleasures offered by a respected old age, such as Duncan had, but which Macbeth made impossible for himself – honour and 'troops of friends'. Cordelia knew this meaning even in saying she loved Lear according to her bond, and Lear himself learned it in the course of the play. Macbeth too learned that life can have a meaning but his being was destroyed in gaining the understanding. He has earned painfully all his understanding. As Gaunt reflected proverbially in his death-bed oration in *Richard II* that 'they breathe truth that breathe their words in pain' (II.i.8), so Macbeth's lesson, won with utmost pain, is uttered with striking clarity.

The moral that would here follow, in the action reading of the play, where Macbeth is motivated by ambition, is 'crime does not pay'. This might, perhaps, work for *Richard III*'s complex action in a simple social frame, but its inappropriateness to the material of *Macbeth* should be clear – because *Macbeth* concerns the principles on which conduct is based, the values, rather than the logic with which they are carried out. Macbeth's failure does not result from his neglecting factors in the process of success; he does in fact succeed in what he asks for and is king for much longer in the playworld's time scale than, say, Lear's retirement. His failure is that he did not conceive how social rewards are *essentially* social – that they exist in the relationships of people – and cannot be achieved individualistically or mechanically, i.e. by seizing the throne. To say 'love me or I'll kill you' destroys the very thing it is trying to create. Macbeth asked for the image, when only the essential thing would be satisfying, to be regal, not just have the throne.

Stylistic argument

Tragedy traditionally involves the fall of a man who is supposed to be good – otherwise there would be little reason to regret his downfall. Such a murderer as Macbeth cannot be good, but in his social desires there is a positive element with which we can remain in sympathy. Like Oedipus answering the riddle of the Sphinx, Macbeth's success is his failure, and his tragedy, again like that of Oedipus, lies in his realisation of what he has done, the destruction of anything that could make his life meaningful. But superficially, in terms of the action alone, the quality that can justify Macbeth as a tragic hero is the recovery of his military bearing, his physical heroism. When he realises the doubleness of the witches' prophecy – Burnam Wood *has* come to Dunsinane and Macduff informs him he was not *born* of woman – it cows his 'better part of man' and he refuses to fight Macduff. That is, until Macduff creates an image of Macbeth's captivity, and that stimulates him to heroic encounter again. Once more he is the man of Lady Macbeth's vision, whose 'better part' is fearless violence:

> Yet I will try the last: before my body
> I throw my warlike shield: lay on, Macduff;
> And damn'd be him that first cries, 'Hold, enough!'
> (V.viii.32–4)

Once again he is 'Bellona's bridegroom', living up to Hamlet's image of Fortinbras's soldiers who 'Go to their graves like beds' (IV.iv.62).

Certainly Shakespeare needs an ending, but if the action of these three lines returns Macbeth to heroic status, it is a very fragile heroism and *Macbeth* signifies nothing. To treat the simplistic value structure tactfully and yet undermine it, Shakespeare turns to stylistic argument.

Shakespeare establishes in *Macbeth*, more than in any other play, his superlative linguistic skill. For example: the difference in poetic character of Banquo's language from Macbeth's, or the use of choric rhetoric in the captain's description of Macbeth's exploits in the second scene, or the perfectly calculated image, at once in keeping with the characters and resounding far beyond them, like Macbeth's strikingly appropriate yet imprecise image of his motive –

> ⸱   I have no spur
> To prick the sides of my intent, but only
> Vaulting ambition, which o'erleaps itself
> And falls on th'other – (I.vii.25–8)

All of these suggest an exceptionally detailed attention to language, so the tone of the final scene of the play must be taken as
intentional and therefore significant. As the cost of the victory
over Macbeth is being assessed, Malcolm expresses some uneasiness: 'I would the friends we miss were safe arriv'd'. Old
Siward makes immediately evident his bluff military character in
answering Malcolm:

> Some must go off; and yet, by these I see,
> So great a day as this is cheaply bought. (V.ix.1,2–3)

He was given a thumbnail characterisation by Malcolm in Act IV,
scene iii: 'An older, and a better soldier, none/ That Christendom
gives out' (IV.iii.191–2). He is the traditional fighting man. But
Siward's bluffness is insensitivity when the focus becomes the
death of his own son. Shakespeare presented his death to the
audience – nine lines in Act V, scene vii, that, as with the sketch
of young Macduff, characterise him as brave, purposeful and
possessed of integrity, if also somewhat precocious. Malcolm tells
Siward his son is missing, and Rosse then announces his death in
terms that, though general, express feeling:

> Your son, my Lord, has paid a soldier's debt:
> He only liv'd but till he was a man;
> The which no sooner had his prowess confirm'd,
> In the unshrinking station where he fought,
> But like a man he died. (V.ix.5–9)

Siward makes a matter-of-fact reply, 'Then he is dead?', to which
Rosse adds a fitting ceremonial tone:

> Ay, and brought off the field. Your cause of sorrow
> Must not be measur'd by his worth, for then
> It hath no end. (V.ix.10–12)

Siward's speeches have no ceremony, they are composed of
reasoning rather than emotional response. When he has assured
himself that his son died fighting, that he was not killed running
away ('Had he his hurts before?' – V.ix.12), he then pronounces:

Why then, God's soldier be he!
Had I as many sons as I have hairs,
I would not wish them to a fairer death:
And so, his knell is knoll'd. (V.ix.13–16)

Malcolm, himself no paragon of sensitivity (as he shows in IV.iii), counters with an immediately emotional response – 'He's worth more sorrow,/ And that I'll spend for him' (V.ix.16–17) – but Shakespeare underscores Siward's attitude by having him reiterate his earlier sentiments:

He's worth no more;
They say he parted well and paid his score:
And so, God be with him! (V.ix.17–19)

Aside from the emphasis on lack of feeling in the interchanges of the characters, Shakespeare gives Siward the crudely articulated 'worth no more / paid his score' rhyme, which reduces life to terms of contract. Siward also utters the most ridiculous pun, 'hairs / heirs', which robs the scene of whatever dignity Rosse's ceremonial language can confer on it, and he parallels this with the crude, nonsensical-sounding 'knell is knoll'd'. The ridiculousness is intentional but it is not comic; it helps determine audience attitude toward the victors, whether or not they are to be given moral approbation. In the argument by style, they are not.

Shakespeare prepares the audience for the stylistic argument of the final scene in Act IV, scene iii. In the three scenes of Act IV he employs theatre's range of techniques of meaning (song excepted) with a skill he equals only in *The Winter's Tale* and *The Tempest*. Scene i has the spectacle of the witches' dumbshow, followed in scene ii by a warm domestic interchange between a witty child and an ironic mother that is charmingly elaborated in the shadow of messengers of danger, releasing its tension only in the brutality of the murder of the mother and child. The scene is both touching and horrific, stretching the responses of the audience. It also relocates the focus of emotion from Macbeth to what his actions mean in terms of people's lives, from tragedy as the heroic deliberation of individuals to tragedy as the concrete sufferings of ordinary people.

The third scene depends on audience response to the second, building on the emotions generated there and making an obvious contrast to it. The first lines signal a change in rhetoric from the homely scale of the preceding scene to the conventional and heroic:

> Let us seek out some desolate shade, and there
> Weep our sad bosoms empty. (IV.iii.1–2)

Malcolm's 'desolate shade' and 'weep our sad bosoms empty' could come from Sidney's *Arcadia* or *The Golden Aphroditis* of John Grange in their literary character, and even Macduff's response shares this quality in its symmetrical relation to Malcolm's words:

> Let us rather
> Hold fast the mortal sword, and like good men
> Bestride our downfall birthdom. (IV.iii.2–4)

The elevation, formality, balance – in short, the conventional rhetorical quality – of Malcolm's discourse in the scene's first hundred and sixty lines emphasise its abstraction. The substance as well as the style seems abstract, as in his list of twelve abstract qualities that comprise the kingly virtues: 'Justice, Verity, Temp'rance, Stableness, Bounty, Perseverance, Mercy, Lowliness, Devotion, Patience, Courage, Fortitude'. These are opposed to the adjectives applied to Macbeth: 'bloody, luxurious, avaricious, false, deceitful, sudden, malicious, smacking of every sin that has a name' (IV.iii.92–4, 57–60). The dialogue is, frankly, boring, but it conveys the difference between abstract traits and the embodied characteristics of the previous scene. The abstractions are part of the distant magic of royalty, Edward the Confessor's curative touching for 'the king's evil' and even Malcolm's virginity.

With the entry of Rosse, however, the character of the scene changes from the abstract–philosophical to the immediate, human–dramatic, for Rosse bears the news of the carnage we have been witness to in the preceding scene. The tension arises from Macduff's coming ever nearer to the disaster of discovery. The content produces tension – we know what has happened and what it will mean to Macduff – but tension is also created through the formal structure, and that lends the subject more importance and gives it a tragic dignity. We know that the revelation will be a disaster that can be delayed but not prevented. Shakespeare manipulates the situation like an angler playing out line and reeling it in. He has Macduff approach discovery when he asks Rosse, 'How does my wife?' (IV.iii.176), but forestalls it through Rosse's evasion of that and the next two inquiries, and his ambiguous 'they were well at peace, when I did leave 'em' (IV.iii.179). Tension is dissipated when Malcolm forecloses questioning with an 'answer' that Siward and 10,000 English soldiers are coming to Scotland's aid, but it mounts again as Rosse returns to the disaster, leading Macduff toward it and then away from it, till Macduff says 'quickly let me have it' (IV.iii.200). Finally Rosse says:

Your castle is surpris'd; your wife, and babes,
Savagely slaughter'd: (IV.iii.204–5)

This blow releases the tension and Macduff starts to crumble under it. But it is so wrenching that he cannot grasp it and must ask again if his children were also killed and, yet again, if his wife was killed.

Malcolm participates in the catastrophe with the same abstract quality as earlier in the scene:

Be comforted:
Let's make us med'cines of our great revenge,
To cure this deadly grief. (IV.iii.213–15)

His narrow range of response and limited sense of humanity are apparent when he tells Macduff, 'Dispute it like a man' (IV.iii.220). Malcolm does not understand that the loss experienced by Macduff is specific and absolute: Macduff cannot 'make it right' by revenge, nor can he be consoled by fine sentiments, any more than Hamlet is comforted to be told death is common. Macduff's response is:

I shall do so;
But I must also feel it as a man (IV.iii.220–1).

The two uses of 'man' here parallel the definitions disputed by Macbeth and Lady Macbeth before the murder of Duncan: humanity and personal fortitude. Shakespeare uses repetition to drive home the point, having Malcolm praise Macduff when his speech turns to retribution: 'This tune goes manly' (IV.iii.235). Macduff's Man earns the title through personal relationships, Malcolm's Man through aggression and stoic insensitivity.

The opposition of definitions of humanity helps answer the vexed question of Macduff's reference when he comments 'He has no children' (IV.iii.216), after Malcolm's suggestion of the curative power of revenge: because Malcolm has no children, he is unable to understand what the loss of a child means to a parent. Shakespeare is showing the *difference* between Malcolm and Macduff rather than their continuity.

The heroic tone of the play's conclusion and Siward's insistent lack of feeling mark a return to the values of the beginning – blood, machismo, blind heroic confrontation. But the insensitivity at the end is worse than that at the beginning because the victors see no contradictions in their attitudes. They have not learned from the experience of the events; Macbeth was the only one who learned, and he is dead. The villain is dead but those who beat him are not the 'good guys', for they show no sense of human richness. They are not personally evil, they are inadequate humans. Polanski adds an illuminating action to the end of his film version of the play (1971) – Malcolm visits the witches. He has not rejected antisocial attitudes, only the overt and violent inhumanity of his predecessor. Lady Macbeth's 'nearest way' has become the mode; the 'efficiency' of ignoring anything that cannot be quantified and of denying the collective nature of humanity dominates the playworld. The contracted world of King Malcolm is the Rome where the next tragedy unfolds itself.

CHAPTER VI

Antony and Cleopatra

The playworld of *Antony and Cleopatra*, though literally Rome, seems to reproduce the qualities that dominated the end of *Macbeth*. The suggestion in Polanski's film of *Macbeth*, when Malcolm visits the witches at the end, is that ultimately there is little distinction between the supposed good and bad personages of the play, and Shakespeare's mockery in the manner of presentation in the final scene suggests that the victors are deficient in the humane understanding possessed even by the villain. They cannot understand that things may contain their opposites and may change their meaning; truth is proved by definition, not by trial.

It is in such a world that *Antony and Cleopatra* opens. Apart from specific, historically important questions raised in regard to the transition from republic to empire, Rome had a traditional value for the audience as a repository of civic order. In *Hamlet*, when Horatio asserts the nobility of his suicidal impulse, he says he is 'more an antique Roman than a Dane' (V.ii.346). From no other setting could such established order be expected – from neither ancient Britain nor Scotland, and certainly not from the Danes, who are, rails Nashe in *Pierce Penniless*, 'bursten-bellied sots' (in *The Unfortunate Traveller and other Works*, p. 77). And it is the very nature of that order that is in question in the play.

In the playworld Rome the new order has already become established; the process of transition, of the new world shattering the old, seen in *Hamlet* and *King Lear*, has already taken place. Unlike *Hamlet* and *King Lear*, the action is not viewed through the values of an earlier order, and in that sense it cannot be seen as a 'corruption' of anything. Yet in the new order the verbal remains of the old system are still present – as with Falstaff, the signals of old values are uttered with indifference to their old meaning. Self-interest is still the principal motivation here, but it can no longer appear in the heroic posture of a radical exception, of an Edmund, for it has become dominant. Now its success is based on adherence to rule. It is the self-interest of the accountant rather than the captain of industry. It is safe, following probabilities and avoiding risk. There is no place for the unique, for feeling, for imagination, for spirit. The world is reduced to bare matter:

> young boys and girls
> Are level now with men: the odds is gone,
> And there is nothing left remarkable
> Beneath the visiting moon. (IV.xv.65–8)

This is the world in which the hero Antony was the last exception, as Cleopatra's lines above express it, a character of old-style heroic mould. He is possessed of the qualities that coloured the Renaissance: an individual centred in himself, fired by his own feelings, who would transform the world to his own desires. Like Castiglione's courtier, he draws his excellence from his personal, inborn qualities, not from practice or labour. He has the grace produced by *sprezzatura*, by nonchalance – the aristocratic spirit that moves effortlessly and unconcernedly above the workaday world. Victory alone does not make the hero – Octavius Caesar is successful but not heroic. The Romans can defeat Antony only through calculation and effort – they have no style. Octavius Caesar fits himself willingly to the demands of his environment. Antony, on the other hand, looms larger than his environment, not subject to measure. His heroism lies in an individuality beyond rule or calculation; he is unique.

Where can such a hero exist? Not in Rome – for Antony to confine his heroism within the limits of Roman calculation is to cease to be a hero. He cannot regain approval from a Rome that is only embarrassed at his individualism, and Rome cannot tolerate a great personage that flouts its very principles, 'A man who is the abstract of all faults/ That all men follow', in the words of Octavius Caesar (I.iv.9–10). The contradiction cannot endure. But the conflict can be postponed; Antony attempts to move the action from the public to the private sphere. Instead of playing the hero on the stage of world affairs, of conquest and government, Antony acts in a domestic world on a heroic scale. He produces from his personal relationship with Cleopatra the same kind of grandeur and intensity as from his heroism in the larger world, and his action is conceived heroically, not in relative values but in the sphere of absolutes. Paradoxically, it is the concern with the heroic that moves the play away from being a character study. The heroic, however much it may strive for absolutes, requires a context, and it is the conflict between the civic order and the qualities of heroism that gives energy to the story Shakespeare adapted. It should also be said that, contrary to its popular reputation, the tragedy is not about love: although love may be the material out of which the story is composed, it provides neither the principle that shapes the plot nor the perspective in which events are viewed. Despite the similar pairing of names in the title, the relationship does not have the same quality as that in *Romeo and Juliet*. Whatever the historical relationship that is reflected in the play, Cleopatra's role is *dramatically* subordinate to Antony's – although she moves independently, the relationship is controlled by choices made in the context of Antony's career. Cleopatra is certainly not a passive character, but her life in the playworld is determined largely by other people's decisions. This is perhaps most obvious in comparison with *Romeo and Juliet*, where the effect of the protagonists on the course of the action is more equal.

Antony's heroism

Shakespeare offers two models of outstanding conduct, Octavius Caesar and Antony. It is difficult to call Caesar heroic – he is no more heroic than the cold and cunning Prince John of 2 *Henry IV* who becomes, in Falstaff's construction, an epitome of civil form without humanity, not unlike Octavius Caesar (IV.iii). Antony, on the other hand, enters the play already a hero – he does not have to achieve that status within the play – but the essence of his heroism is not immediately obvious. Pompey confirms his military excellence, saying that, compared with Caesar and Lepidus, 'his soldiership/ Is twice the other twain' (II.i.34–5), and Caesar himself praises Antony's hardiness, his ability to withstand difficulties (I.iv.55–71). Even Maecenas, who has expressed characteristic Roman reservations about Antony's conduct, makes a final judgement of his heroism in relation to Caesar when Caesar is reflecting on Antony's death:

> When such a spacious mirror's set before him,
> He needs must see himself. (V.i.34–5)

Antony displays also the Roman virtues of honesty and directness. These are whipped into a heroic posture of supreme devotion to truth:

> Who tells me true, though in his tale lie death,
> I hear him as he flatter'd. (I.ii.95–6)

But this sentiment, expressed again in a different image of weeds and ploughing a few lines later (106–8), is a kind of schoolboy virtue, something Polonius could have held up to Laertes.

Antony's magnanimity is the counterpart of his romantic posture in regard to truth. He is magnanimous in the literal and classical sense of being great-souled – he is above petty things and has a largeness of spirit. This quality is clearly illustrated by his sending Enobarbus's treasure him after when he leaves to join Caesar.

> Go, Eros, send his treasure after, do it,
> Detain no jot, I charge thee: write to him –
> I will subscribe – gentle adieus, and greetings;
> Say, that I wish he never find more cause
> To change a master. O, my fortunes have
> Corrupted honest men. Despatch. – Enobarbus.
>   (IV.v.12–17)

Antony presents Enobarbus's behaviour not as a failure of relationship between the two men, but as an aspect of his own misfortunes, a larger context of the fortunes of men where Enobarbus is seen also as a victim. Antony does not descend from his Olympian vantage point to blame Enobarbus.

Antony's grand behaviour is accompanied by a vulgar heroism, the opposite of the Roman restraint, a kind of carnival excess and self-indulgence – e.g., the reported eight wild boars roasted whole at a breakfast for only twelve people, which Enobarbus says 'was but as a fly by an eagle' (II.ii.179–81), the atmosphere of sex and sensuality, and the intemperate drinking which disables the former (as *Macbeth*'s porter explained it). Caesar, on the other hand, clearly distances himself from such lack of control and objects to getting drunk – 'It's monstrous labour when I wash my brain/ And it grows fouler' (II.vii.97–8). Antony's excess, however, is more than physical appetite or a mindless vulgarity; it is part of a style, a physical but symbolic imposition of the will on the environment. It is an individuality that defies convention.

The counterpart can be seen in Cleopatra's behaviour as described by Enobarbus. Although the famous description of the barge on the river of Cydnus offers a more refined, ordered, artificial consciousness than that suggested earlier in regard to Antony, the quality that is specifically her heroism is given by Enobarbus only *after* he has glutted the imaginations of Maecenas and Agrippa with the images of luxury. Thus, by the structuring of Enobarbus's presentation (as well as in analysis), this becomes what distinguishes her:

> I saw her once
> Hop forty paces through the public street,
> And having lost her breath, she spoke, and panted,
> That she did make defect perfection,
> And, breathless, power breathe forth. (II.ii.228–32)

Enobarbus continues the description of her personal power:

> Age cannot wither her, nor custom stale
> Her infinite variety: other women cloy
> The appetites they feed, but she makes hungry,
> Where most she satisfies. For vilest things
> Become themselves in her, that the holy priests
> Bless her, when she is riggish. (II.ii.235–40)

Cleopatra is not distinguished by her sensuality but by being able to engage in public behaviour unsuitable for a queen and totally lacking in aristocratic dignity, behaviour which she makes seem not only appropriate but honourable as well. This is Cleopatra being a standard-setter, not a follower. It is this quality which attracts Antony so powerfully to her. Cleopatra's qualities are beyond the comprehension of Roman Maecenas; they are features of display – the side-show of the human circus – but not qualities for a relationship. He is certain that Octavia's modesty is preferable (II.ii.241–3).

Antony's heroism is beyond material exploits – it involves the specifically humane, the excess of the whole being, rather than hypertrophy of one aspect. Thus Cleopatra's praise of the dead Antony – 'his delights/ Were dolphin-like, they show'd his back above/ The element they lived in' (V.ii.88–90) – makes him exceptional as a human spirit, not as fighter, reveller, or whatever. It is the largeness of his soul – 'For his bounty,/ There was no winter in't' (V.ii.86–7) – that is heroic. Even off the world stage, when he might be considered to retreat from the public responsibility of 'the rang'd empire' into the private sphere of a relationship with Cleopatra – 'Here is my space' – he displays the same heroic attitude, saying as he embraces Cleopatra, 'the nobleness of life/ Is to do thus'. He says in this they are 'peerless' (I.i.34,36–7,40). Because it is conceived of heroically, even the domestic becomes heroic. The heroism is in the style, not the content.

Antony is *sui generis* – unique, large and powerful. He is not subject to measure or categories. This is most clearly illustrated by his opening lines, in response to Cleopatra's demand to say how much he loves her: 'There's beggary in the love that can be reckon'd' (I.i.15). Heroic love, the only love worth so designating, is beyond calculation and beyond the material. (This position is reminiscent of the love test in *Lear*, where Goneril and Regan quantified love and Cordelia's love was incalculable.) Antony's heroic view of love is juxtaposed with Philo's description of Antony's former greatness:

> his captain's heart
> Which in the scuffles of great fights hath burst
> The buckles on his breast. (I.i.6–8)

Philo's vision of the heroic does not rise beyond the material – Arnold Schwarzenegger could do the same. Antony's military behaviour may itself be potentially heroic but the description given by Philo lacks spirit and fails to be heroic. It is this very material-bound consciousness of Rome that makes Antony's existence as a hero impossible.

Roman character

The problem posed for Antony by Roman consciousness, and which constrains his heroic being, is not so much that its values are in conflict with his own – like, say, Athens in opposition to Sparta – but that it is extremely limited. The excitement offered by Cleopatra is an individuality that defies pigeon-holing. Her unregal behaviour is not the same as 'transgression' or violation of boundaries which, paradoxically, emphasises the significance of limits; Cleopatra's actions, on the contrary, deny altogether the *relevance* of boundaries. Boundaries may be relevant to a rule-directed consciousness, but not to the expression of a free self. Rome insists on everything being one thing or another, without overlap; it is intolerant of confusion or lack of clarity. Gender divisions are an obvious instance. Caesar is critical of Antony because he does not follow his proper sexual role: he

> is not more manlike
> Than Cleopatra; nor the queen of Ptolemy
> More womanly than he. (I.iv.5-7)

The first time Shakespeare recognises such a gender critique is in *Macbeth* where Lady Macbeth annihilates the category of man-as-human by distributing the 'human' entirely between male and female, between aggressive and passive. Hamlet suffers no such gender anxiety, and the Elizabethan world view, as presented by Sir Philip Sidney in *The Arcadia* (c.1584), saw the complete human soul as containing both male and female. In fact, Sidney's hero Pyrocles disguises himself as an Amazon without damage to his integrity.

The order of Rome is not related to the functioning of relationships in their essence but, like bureaucracy, is concerned with adherence to rules, which allows no place for the individuality of the hero. Lepidus, encouraging the restoration of good relations between Caesar and Antony, asks Enobarbus to persuade Antony to mildness and says, ''Tis not a time/ For private stomaching.' He reiterates the principle of order: 'But small to greater matters must give way.' Enobarbus's definitive response, 'Not if the small come first', asserts that order is not a matter of abstract precedence but must take particular cases into account (II.ii.8–12).

Antony himself speaks of needing to break his 'Egyptian fetters' or lose himself in 'dotage' (I.ii.113–14) and he makes one attempt to adopt Roman attitudes, saying to Octavia that he will be straightforward with her and all shall 'be done by the rule' (II.iii.7). But there is no possibility of squeezing the hero into the narrow Roman pattern. As Enobarbus comments on the marriage:

> But you shall find the band that seems to tie their friendship together will be the very strangler of their amity

and adds, 'Octavia is of a holy, cold and still conversation.' Menas, another choric figure – indifferently honest, martial and Roman – recognises this as an embodiment of Roman virtue, which, therefore, must be a positive bond in the relationship: 'Who would not have his wife so?', he asks. Enobarbus answers, 'Not he that himself is not so; which is Mark Antony' (II.vi.117–23). Roman virtue is privative, opposed to the positive, expansive, humane attitude taken by Antony.

Antony's sensuality, his attention to the particular at the expense of the general, his individualism, are seen in the Roman perspective as 'dotage'. Antony even reflects some of this himself. When he says he needs to break off 'from this enchanting queen' (I.ii.125), there is a suggestion of a real world to which he must return, that the relationship with Cleopatra is carnival. Emotional response that affects behaviour is seen as degenerate. The distinction between mechanical human functioning and socialised feeling–response echoes the argument between Macbeth and Lady Macbeth over the humane and aggressive definitions of man. But whereas Lady Macbeth was encouraging her husband to a behaviour that was regarded as extraordinary and antisocial in the playworld, the Roman norm, in its lack of reflection and feeling, accepts a mode of conduct not far from what she advocated. Therefore, Antony, acting in response to feeling, is seen as regressing, and Demetrius must 'hope/ Of better deeds to-morrow' (I.i.61–2).

This individualism has no place in the Roman argument – it is either unrecognised or irrelevant, and can only hinder the success of the person who possesses it. As the soothsayer explains to Antony, his spirit is 'Noble, courageous, high, unmatchable,/ Where Caesar's is not' (II.iii.19–20), but where Caesar's *is*, Antony's is overpowered. Its excellent and individual qualities cannot withstand the monolithic order of Rome. Antony's cause is hopeless; attractive, warm, human – but hopeless.

Image and actuality

Shakespeare occasionally signals a material reality that underlies the posturing. Enobarbus, evaluating the political situation that heralds the war between Caesar and Antony, says:

> world, thou has a pair of chaps, no more
> And throw between them all the food thou hast,
> They'll grind the one the other. (III.v.13–15)

There is little possibility of humane culture on so hostile a basis, but the *dramatic* concern of the play, for the most part, is focused on the attitudes that result from this.

What makes Antony's cause hopeless is not the limited prospects of material success – were Antony to measure things in that way he would already have conceded Caesar's victory. The problem is that Antony's understanding is inexpressible (and therefore socially non-existent) in the language of Rome. This is not for lack of appropriate words, but because the words have ceased to have real meaning. The word has become separated from the world to which it was once attached and, as in a world re-created by advertising, the image serves as the equivalent of the actuality.

The most obvious instance of this is certainly a direct contradiction between the reality and its representation. Thus Ventidius advises Silius that a subordinate who is too successful in carrying out military tasks damages his superior's image. Thereby the basis of the general's superiority is rendered doubtful and his favour towards his officer is put at risk. Ventidius's own success might endanger the good opinion Antony has of him:

Caesar and Antony have ever won
More in their officer than person. (III.i.16–17)

But this contradiction is perhaps most widespread in the Roman
formality and orientation towards rules whereby empty gestures
and forms without substance are acceptable. While juxtaposition
of form with empty reality in the plot shows this, it is most
sharply focused in irony. Antony, for example, weaves from
nothing a witty answer to the vacant Lepidus who drunkenly
demands of him, 'What manner o' thing is your crocodile?'
Antony replies:

> It is shap'd, sir, like itself, and it is as broad as it hath breadth: it is just
> so high as it is, and moves with it own organs. It lives by that which
> nourisheth it, and the elements once out of it, it transmigrates.

The mockery is given dramatic emphasis through repetition:
Lepidus asks, 'What colour is it of?', to which Antony replies, 'Of
it own colour too' (II.vii.40–46).

Lepidus accepts the mere *form* of a definition as a definition.
This passage has the shallow amusement of most drunken
interchanges, but Lepidus continues the confusion of image and
actuality in his sober analysis. When Caesar attacks Antony as 'the
abstract of all faults', Lepidus defends him by saying, 'His faults,
in him, seem as the spots of heaven,/ More fiery by night's
blackness' (I.iv.12–13). Since the heroic quality is image, the
faults are only part of the image and are, therefore, different from
substantial faults; and the simile confirms in image Antony's
'heavenly' heroic quality.

More important is the mockery of heroic postures by Agrippa
and Enobarbus because, unlike Lepidus, they are witty and
knowledgeable. Shakespeare has them play with rhetorical forms
of praise, making their judgement a sophisticated one that, like
the ironic playing of Falstaff, debases the standard as well as the
thing compared:

> *Agr.* What, are the brothers parted?
> *Eno.* They have despatch'd with Pompey, he is gone,
>   The other three are sealing. Octavia weeps
>   To part from Rome; Caesar is sad, and Lepidus,
>   Since Pompey's feast, as Menas says, is troubled
>   With the green-sickness.

> *Agr.* 'Tis a noble Lepidus.
> *Eno.* A very fine one: O, how he loves Caesar!
> *Agr.* Nay, but how dearly he adores Mark Antony!
> *Eno.* Caesar! Why he's the Jupiter of men.
> *Agr.* What's Antony? The god of Jupiter.
> *Eno.* Spake you of Caesar? How, the nonpareil?
> *Agr.* O Antony, O thou Arabian bird!
> *Eno.* Would you praise Caesar, say 'Caesar,' go no further.
> *Agr.* Indeed he plied them both with excellent praises.
> *Eno.* But he loves Caesar best, yet he loves Antony:
> Hoo! hearts, tongues, figures, scribes, bards, poets cannot
> Think, speak, cast, write, sing, number, hoo,
> His love to Antony. But as for Caesar,
> Kneel down, kneel down, and wonder.
> *Agr.* Both he loves.
> *Eno.* They are his shards, and he their beetle, so:
> (III.ii.1–20)

Despite the efforts of editors to find a meaning for 'shards' that preserves the triumvirs' dignity, it is clear from the rhetorical structure that Agrippa and Enobarbus mock their masters with praise, capping the mockery by presenting them as the element where the dung beetle finds protection – in effect saying that they are both turds – thereby giving a verbal recognition of their baseness. Shakespeare emphasises it through structure: it is the scene following Ventidius's warning about the difference between the expectations of military performance and actuality in the world of real practice.

The severest indication of the predominance of image over actuality in Rome is the incident where Menas suggests to Pompey that he slit the triumvirs' throats while they are feasting on board Pompey's ship. Pompey would have liked it done but cannot *knowingly* accept it (like Macbeth, in his wife's estimation, being willing to win unfairly but not to play false – I.v.21–2). Pompey acts on the basis of 'honour' – but the concept is very much deteriorated here:

> Ah, this thou shouldst have done,
> And not have spoke on't! In me 'tis villainy,
> In thee, 't had been good service. Thou must know,
> 'Tis not my profit that does lead mine honour;
> Mine honour, it. Repent that e'er thy tongue

> Hath so betray'd thine act. Being done unknown,
> I should have found it afterwards well done,
> But must condemn it now. Desist, and drink.
>   (II.vii.72–9)

Pompey's concern is more image than actuality; he illustrates the degeneration of Rome. The action, not being consequential in terms of plot (it does not alter the course of events, despite its potential to do so), serves to reflect the condition of Rome: honour has declined to the mere image of honour.

Antony is part of the same world, equally affected by the confusion of image and actuality (even if more tastefully so). He rejects reason in accepting Caesar's dare to fight by sea (III,vii) and Enobarbus comments on his deranged heroic image:

> Now he'll outstare the lightning; to be furious
> Is to be frighted out of fear, and in that mood
> The dove will peck the estridge; and I see still,
> A diminution in our captain's brain
> Restores his heart; when valour preys on reason,
> It eats the sword it fights with: I will seek
> Some way to leave him. (III.xiii.195–201)

Enobarbus must leave Antony because Antony insists on destroying himself, repulsing reason for self-image. When discourse is juxtaposed with action Antony's words become mere empty rhetoric. Thus, responding to the reported death of Cleopatra, he waxes heroic in his speech:

> O, cleave, my sides!
> Heart, once be stronger than thy continent,
> Crack thy frail case! (IV.xiv.39–41)

Though he asks that the spirit be stronger than the flesh and, as 'heart', burst the body, yet he is unable to kill himself with his sword. Eros, however, from whom he asks assistance, nobly chooses to slay himself rather than kill his master (IV.xiv.84–95). Antony's rhetoric is hollow.

The greatness of heart, Antony's spiritual heroism, narrows in focus; rather than the great spirit guiding the whole man, it eventually seems to be a case of the spirit *only*, of an ideal of no force in relation to matters of the material world of business, of conventional heroism, of social doing:

> Let Rome in Tiber melt, and the wide arch
> Of the rang'd empire fall! (I.i.33–4)

This is a noble attitude, but it is no more than attitude. Antony's posturing is emphasised by Enobarbus. When Antony says they must leave Egypt, Enobarbus replies that their departure would 'kill' all their women. Antony insists 'I must be gone' (I.ii.133), and Enobarbus then makes an ironic integration of the love-sick and the world-historical postures:

> Under a compelling occasion let women die: it were a pity to cast them away for nothing, though between them and a great cause, they should be esteemed nothing. (I.ii.134–7)

The inflation of Roman rhetoric alters what Antony *is*; he too has become part of the rhetoric. The image Antony puts forward is certainly more attractive than the Roman one, but it is not reality in opposition to an image; it is a counter-image.

This quality of image-as-opposition is most obvious, however, in Cleopatra. To see her as a creature of image is not to deny her heroic quality. She knows Caesar requires a living Cleopatra to maintain an image of nobility. Proculeius had said to her:

> Cleopatra,
> Do not abuse my master's bounty, by
> The undoing of yourself: let the world see
> His nobleness well acted, which your death
> Will never let come forth. (V.ii.42–6)

Her refusal to accept the image she imagines Caesar will make of her in captivity – a staging of a drunken Antony and 'Some squeaking Cleopatra boy my greatness/ I' the posture of a whore' (V.ii.219–20) – is an assertion of values. The image contains a reality of values and aspirations, which in one sense is more real than the material world in which she moves (like Macbeth's 'And nothing is, but what is not' – I.iii.142).

Unlike the Romans, Cleopatra is well aware of the distinction between image and actuality, and this allows her playing with image to be enjoyable in the same way that it is in the mature comedies. Her posturing is enjoyed as posturing, as the recognition of a range of possible ways of being, in the same spirit as *As You Like It* or *Twelfth Night*. It is this element of active individuality, of imagination, delight, energy, feeling and wit that makes Cleopatra irresistible for Antony. The play of artifice can be seen in the way she re-characterises Octavia from the beginning of the messenger's report – not being as tall as Cleopatra and being low-voiced are transformed into 'dull of tongue, and dwarfish!' (III.iii.16) – a sport in which the messenger himself joins. Language is play, as in Act I, scene iii, where despite some five attempts in nearly thirty lines Antony is unable to get a word in because Cleopatra is dominating the field, like the unruly Hotspur conspiring in Act I, scene iii, of 1 *Henry IV*. The specific discourse is of much less import than the interrelations seen in the domination of the conversational situation. Rhetoric is the medium in which Cleopatra exists.

All the feigning, the pretended dyings, are rhetorical in serving primarily to evoke a response rather than alter the action (in contrast, say, to Rosalind or Viola whose disguise is intended initially as a protection). Rhetoric need not be hollow, but Cleopatra ultimately takes a position that can never be more than mere posture. She says, for example, that she should attack the gods for stealing Antony (IV.xv.75–8) and rails on Fortune:

> No, let me speak, and let me rail so high,
> That the false huswife Fortune break her wheel,
> Provok'd by my offence. (IV.xv.43–5)

Marlowe gives Tamburlaine a similar statement in relation to Fortune – 'I hold the Fates bound fast in iron chains,/ And with my hand turn Fortune's wheel about' (*The Complete Plays*, ed. J. B. Steane, 1973: Penguin, Harmondsworth; I.ii.174–5) – but the grand rhetorical character of that play makes it quite clear that incident and speech are intended at a metaphorical level rather than being a literal statement, which would suggest paranoid delusion (we do not expect to see Tamburlaine turning Fortune's wheel). Like Antony calling for his heart to burst his sides, Cleopatra's relation to Fortune suggests something much more instrumental than Tamburlaine's and its actual impossibility is therefore more disappointing. She calls for something where the action seems possible but the context makes it in fact impossible, and it is therefore hollow. Rhetoric here remains merely rhetoric.

Nostalgia

When Cleopatra praises the dead Antony to Dolabella, speaking of his bounty without winter and his dolphin-like delights that rise above their element, she asks, 'Think you there was, or might be such a man/ As this I dreamt of?' He replies succinctly, 'Gentle madam, no' (V.ii.93–4). The hyperbolic paradoxical quality in Cleopatra's praise here is of the same sort as Antony's own in 'There's beggary in the love that can be reckon'd' at the play's opening; but now, at the play's end, the paradox seems to reside more in the reality itself than in the phrasing in which it is represented. This is the impossibility of nostalgia. It is a world that never was, created out of the desires of the present and projected onto the past.

The content of the play's nostalgia is the humane quality that diffuses the representation, how things are pictured. Enobarbus has a subordinate position which allows him to make informed commentary on the action without taking responsibility for events. He is thus well placed to exercise a constant irony, and the humane values that inform his irony produce a nostalgic charm. His wit brings together past and present, again in a manner not unlike that of Falstaff, employing an 'antique' perspective to view the impoverished present. His occasional literalness also exposes the emptiness of the rhetoric of courtesy. Thus, after Pompey's defeat in negotiation, Enobarbus and Menas engage in a dialogue of almost music-hall character:

> *Eno.* You have done well by water.
> *Men.* And you by land.
> *Eno.* I will praise any man that will praise me, though it cannot be denied what I have done by land.
> (II.vi.86–9)

Enobarbus can speak beyond the word; and the word is richer for the sense of a human context. The skill and consciousness displayed in bringing together contradictory elements, in seeing

both image and reality in their contradictory qualities, are the
mark of Enobarbus's outstanding humanity. His style distinguishes him as part of the old world, and from that perspective
he views the hollowness of the new.

Enobarbus displays contradictions not through logic but
through verbal style. Thus, after the news of Fulvia's death, he
says to Antony:

> this grief is crown'd with consolation, your old smock brings forth a
> new petticoat, and indeed the tears live in an onion, that should water
> this sorrow. (I.ii.165–8)

The single phrase 'this grief is crown'd with consolation' has the
form of condolence, which is shown to be no more than form by
the 'crown'd with consolation', the content of which is at odds
with the form. The hollowness Enobarbus presents is a sign of
social decline, but still there is pleasure in his witty construction.
With a charming manner more like Touchstone than Lear's fool,
he serves a reality function.

But the richness of the past that Enobarbus conveys is almost
by definition something that does not exist in the reality of the
present, and it is missing also from the Roman imagination.
When Decretas tells him of Antony's death, Caesar senses an
inadequacy of response which is also the inability to find an
adequate image:

> The breaking of so great a thing should make
> A greater crack. The round world
> Should have shook lions into civil streets,
> And citizens to their dens. The death of Antony
> Is not a single doom, in the name lay
> A moiety of the world. (V.i.14–19)

The thinking is materialistic – the language recognises only the
failure of the material, without displaying imagination or richness
of spirit.

Unlike *Hamlet*, *Macbeth* or even *King Lear*, *Antony and
Cleopatra* does not produce the sense of contradiction at the
ending, where the picture of the present turning into the future
cannot quite live up to the grandeur of what has preceded it. This
is probably because the positive aspects of *Antony and Cleopatra*

were never made part of the reality of the playworld; they remained an image of what had once been, a twilight of the remembered past. The defeat of humane attitudes by soulless calculation is inevitable – the image is not a substitute for the reality. This sunset vision was warming but it could not last.

The sense of outrage present in *Hamlet* and *King Lear* and of frustration in *Macbeth* is not present in *Antony and Cleopatra*. It offers a quieter social critique, but it remains a critique none the less. Caesar's shrewd and cold placing of Antony's former allies and dependents in the front of the battle is juxtaposed by Shakespeare with Enobarbus's reflection on the excellence of Antony and how, having left Antony, he can no longer live:

> I have done ill,
> Of which I do accuse myself so sorely,
> That I will joy no more. (IV.vi.18–20)

Broken off from the social grouping that gave him definition, Enobarbus is as good as dead. The recognition that individual being derives from the social whole perishes with Enobarbus and the other survivors of the old world. The present – Rome – cannot understand the virtue that is the subject of the nostalgia. Not only is heroism impossible in Rome, but the concept that explains Antony is no longer possible in Roman understanding, because it has been driven out by its shadow. As in the complacent acceptance of deteriorating conduct, where people who murder in self-interest can still be regarded as 'good', which causes Hamlet's rage, so 'hero' is no longer understandable; the social meaning has changed. The tragedy of *Antony and Cleopatra* is the loss of shared humanity. And it is, therefore, a diminution of humanity itself, a decline which goes even lower in *Coriolanus*.

CHAPTER VII

Coriolanus
and *Timon of Athens*

Coriolanus is concerned with honour. The whole existence of the hero is directed toward winning honour through military prowess. Like Macbeth, whose social worth in the beginning of the tragedy is established by his slaughter of enemies, Coriolanus's single-minded destruction of the foes of Rome gives him a claim to public regard. The number of his wounds serves as an index of his excellence and his scars are held as signs of honour.

This concern with honour may suggest a continuity of the attitudes and values expressed in *Antony and Cleopatra*, but the vision is narrowed, and the importance of the spirit has diminished as materialism becomes more dominant. In *Antony and Cleopatra* character cannot be measured by wounds. 'If I lose mine honour,/ I lose myself' (III.iv.22–3), says Antony to Octavia, a statement with which Coriolanus would probably have to agree, but between Antony and Coriolanus the terms have changed their value: 'honour', 'lose', even 'mine' and 'self' shift in their meaning. Antony says that his self is defined by honour; i.e., his individual being depends on a public relationship, which is honour. The self is part of a shared, a social, nature; and his individuality is made significant by its connection with society. His honour, then, can be said to be his not absolutely but only in a conditional way; it depends on a public. For Coriolanus, however, his self exists independently of everything else; his honour is therefore his own. It does not depend on the public and cannot be taken away by alteration of public regard; whereas for Antony the honour is *in* the public relationship and cannot exist apart from it. There can be for Antony no honour in isolation; for Coriolanus there can.

Shakespeare's picture of this changed perception of honour marks a further disintegration of the social fabric. Whereas earlier tragedies – *Hamlet*, *King Lear*, *Macbeth* – dealt with an active conflict between social and individual orientations, after *Antony and Cleopatra* – in *Coriolanus* and *Timon of Athens* – the problem is no longer conflict but the inability to recognise social qualities, the blindness of seeing and understanding only in personal terms. *Coriolanus* and *Timon of Athens* are the last moments in the collapse of a late medieval vision that saw people as connected to each other, and they explore the question of whether humanity is possible independent of that connection.

Whereas in *King Lear* Shakespeare's concerns are clearly highlighted by the dramatic action, and *Macbeth*, *Hamlet* and *Antony and Cleopatra* can at least be understood in terms of the action, the last tragedies depend very heavily on verbalised interpretation. The significance of what happens depends on the way it is contextualised. The context that seems most appropriate to me is that developed in the earlier tragedies – the relation between individual and social being. There is a further difficulty with the last two tragedies: they have little in them that is attractive. Whereas *Hamlet*, *King Lear*, *Macbeth* and *Antony and Cleopatra* all had enough richness of humanity to ensure a degree of positive response from the audience, there is little in *Coriolanus* or *Timon of Athens* for an audience to warm to – e.g., love, longing for the affection of society, pursuit of justice, that make for positive feeling. In that sense they have nearly exhausted the possibilities of conventional tragedy (where we are moved by the necessary but not deserved downfall of a 'good' person, i.e., a person with whom we share some values). The borderline between the animal and human is interesting but, with such an impoverished humanity, it generates little feeling. The major tragedies, however disastrous their conclusion, can provide intense satisfaction from producing in the audience in the end an exciting clarity, a sense of what should have been; but *Coriolanus* and *Timon* are cold. The world of reduced humanity takes its toll on the tragedies themselves.

Coriolanus

It is clear that there is something very wrong with the State from the beginning of *Coriolanus*. The populace, suffering famine and

complaining of hoarded grain stocks, are on the verge of
rebellion. Insurrection has in fact begun – 'The other side
o'th'city is risen: why stay we prating here?' (I.i.46–7). Even
though there is still a city and still a social order, it is strained to
breaking point. The disaster is not just impending but, according
to the people, has already arrived. Thus when Menenius Agrippa
arrives to calm matters and asks, 'Why masters, my good friends,
mine honest neighbours,/ Will you undo yourselves?', the First
Citizen replies: 'We cannot sir, we are undone already'
(I.i.61–3).

The understanding Lear gains on the heath, that need is a
problem of government, is no longer thought to be relevant:
authority rules without reference to individual need, and social
worth has become a correlative of wealth:

> *First Citizen.* We are accounted poor citizens, the patricians good. What
> authority surfeits on would relieve us. If they would yield us but
> the superfluity while it were wholesome, we might guess they
> relieved us humanely; but they think we are too dear . . . our
> sufferance is a gain to them. (I.i.14–21)

Competition, not justice, is the principle; no one is going to 'shake
the superflux to them, and show the Heavens more just' (*King
Lear*, III.iv.35–6). And there is no reason why they should, in
Coriolanus's view: 'They ne'er did service for't' (III.i.121).

Shakespeare pictures a real divergence of interest between
plebians and patricians, but the sense of corruption is not located
in one group or the other – it affects the whole society. The
hunger of the plebians does not give them dignity; they are
unprincipled, easily swayed, and lacking logic. Shakespeare discredits them through the superficiality of the rhetoric he has the
First Citizen utter when he continues the speech begun above:

> Let us revenge this with our pikes, ere we become rakes. For the gods
> know, I speak this in hunger for bread, not in thirst for revenge.
> (I.i.21–4)

The facile pairings of pikes/rakes and hunger/thirst have none
of the bite of the parallel scene that opens *Julius Caesar*, and the
easy rhetoric distances through formality the causes of the
insurrection.

Sicinius and Brutus, the tribunes of the people, display a more powerful understanding than the populace, but they too are pictured as corrupt – self-seeking rather than merely struggling for factional advantage. They display wit, but it is cynical: when Sicinius justifies popular dislike of Coriolanus on the ground that 'Nature teaches beasts to know their friends', Menenius asks, 'Pray you, who does the wolf love?', to which Sicinius replies, 'The lamb' (II.i.5–7).

Menenius, the most civil representative of the Senate, is also given a taint of corruption. His salutation of the crowd as 'my good friends, mine honest neighbours' is oily condescension, and the belly fable, his rhetorical coup, also assumes an offensive character. The tale is given only briefly in Plutarch, but Shakespeare elaborates it over the space of sixty-six lines (I.i.88–153). It is not only used cynically by Menenius to emphasise the incompetence and absolute dependence of the plebians, but it serves as well, like epic simile, to characterise the action of the play. In Plutarch the tale is so short as to offer hardly more than a logical parallel, an analogy that justifies the belly as serving a function benefiting the whole body. In the play the elaboration is sufficient for the story to stand as a model for the State. It is a variant of the traditional parallel between the physical body and the body politic, with the belly here developed as the ruling class:

> The Senators of Rome are this good belly,
> And you the mutinous members . . .
> > you shall find
> No public benefit which you receive
> But it proceeds or comes from them to you,
> And no way from yourselves. (I.i.147–53)

The traditional view has here been inverted: the belly becomes, as it were, the head. The body politic is corrupted.

There is no relief from this corruption throughout the play. No oppositional outlook is offered, even at the level of the nostalgia of *Antony and Cleopatra*. There are no good guys. Virgilia, the wife of Coriolanus, expresses values that are more social but her timorous character prevents them serving as a positive statement. None of the characters is attractive. Menenius has wit but no charm, and even the one child in the play is constructed as repulsive. The Volsces are no better than the Romans; the Second Conspirator dismisses the Volscian plebians with choric authority when they cheer Coriolanus:

> And patient fools,
> Whose children he hath slain, their base throats tear
> With giving him glory. (V.vi.52–4)

The changeability they share with the Roman plebians is seen again when, some seventy lines later, they support the condemnation of Coriolanus by Aufidius's faction:

> Tear him to pieces! Do it presently!
> He killed my son! My daughter! He killed my
> cousin Marcus! He killed my father! (V.vi.120–2)

And Aufidius's servants, who after mistaking Coriolanus for a poor man when he comes in disguise to Aufidius's house, seek to justify their cowardice by saying such things as,

> I had thought to have strucken him with a cudgel; and yet my mind gave me his clothes made a false report of him. (IV.v.150–3)

There is no Falstaffian transformation of reality here – only weakness and pretension.

As in *Antony and Cleopatra*, another index of social deterioration is the increasing importance of social forms over their actual content. The honour accorded Coriolanus's wounds is abstracted from a military actuality. Although Virgilia cannot repress her 'Oh no, no, no' at the mention of her husband's wounds, Volumnia insists on the desirability of wounds: I thank the gods for't', and Menenius makes a slogan of them: 'every gash was an enemy's grave' (II.i.119,120,154–55). Coriolanus himself enacts an emblematic scene that serves no purpose beyond revealing the contradiction between gratitude as a formal response and its lack of genuine content. He 'begs' the freedom of a Volscian prisoner who had given him hospitality. Comeinius is moved and says, 'Were he the butcher of my son, he should/Be free as is the wind' (I.ix.86–87). But when Lartius asks his name, Coriolanus says:

> By Jupiter, forgot!
> I am weary, yea, my memory is tired;
> Have we no wine here? (I.ix.88–90)

But the dominance of the form over the immediacy of experience is not a source of wit as it is in *Antony and Cleopatra*. There is no Enobarbus to provide an ironic vision of the action and whatever amusement Shakespeare generates through hollow forms in *Coriolanus* is at the expense of the characters. When, for example, Menenius tries to approach Coriolanus's Volscian camp, his metaphors are misunderstood: when he talks poetically about their 'captain' (meaning Coriolanus), they think of their Volscian leader of that rank, and he is forced to speak by the letter – 'I mean thy general' (V.ii.50–3). Similarly, the compass of traditional values is narrowed and spiritual or social attitudes are reduced to the bare materiality of their embodiment. Thus Valeria, chivvying Virgilia to leave her needlework and go out and be sociable, says:

> You would be another Penelope; yet they say, all the yarn she spun in Ulysses' absence did but fill Ithaca full of moths. (I.iii.82–4)

The model of Greek wit and faithfulness becomes no more than something materially useless.

In such a context it becomes questionable whether or not the focal points of public affection have meaning. 'If any think brave death outweighs bad life,/ And that his country's dearer than himself' (I.vi.71–72), Coriolanus says when he calls for volunteers from among Cominius's soldiers; but what does dearness of 'country' mean? Do these men share the same country as the plebians of the first scene? Coriolanus is not being cynical; it is just that there is a breakdown of shared values. Coriolanus is untouched by the complexities of state Shakespeare elaborated in *Henry V*.

The breakdown of public values and the disintegration of rules of conduct generalised beyond the individual – i.e. principles – means that the social collective is no longer functioning. We are shown the collapse of both the material state and the consciousness that reflects it. What remains, both materially and in consciousness, is the individual. The social disintegration is evident, but it is made significant *for the tragedy* – i.e., affects action – in the way that individuals themselves exhibit the disintegration, in the way that what was social becomes personal. It is through Coriolanus's lack of understanding that we can grasp the loss of socialisation in the playworld. Octavius Caesar, in comparison, even if not himself very socialised, recognises that he must deal with a world running within conventions and rules of social behaviour, and Menenius, no admirer of the plebians, recognises they must be dealt with according to the conventions of civility. Thus when Coriolanus's anger destroys his appeal for popular support for his consulship, Menenius damns the plebians but says of Coriolanus, 'Could he not speak 'em fair?' (III.i.261). No: it would have required of him a higher principle by which his own behaviour would be ordered; Coriolanus can understand only in terms of himself.

This failing is also signalled in the play by the stress placed on his pride, even from the opening interchange where the First Citizen says he could speak well of Coriolanus's service to his country 'but that he pays himself with being proud' (I.i.32–3). Pride, however, is not just the inflated sense of one's own worth to which it is often reduced in late-twentieth-century consciousness. For the Renaissance, its importance was signalled by being treated seriously as the first of the seven deadly sins. This is reflected in conventional representations, e.g., Pride leads the team that draws Lucifera's carriage in Book I of Spenser's *Faerie Queene*, but pride was also understood as something that made possible the exercise of other sins. It encompasses an attitude of independence: of needing no one else, of being indebted to no one else, and of seeing one's own concerns as central to the world. Edmund, in his famous 'bastard' speech where he recognises Nature as his goddess (*King Lear*, I.ii.1–22), is the model of such an attitude. The principles of behaviour that follow from this kind of pride are based on one's own interests, not on anything social; it regards the social as unnecessary except as material through which to realise its own desires. Pride goes before the other sins because it reckons no responsibility save to itself; and, because it subordinates everything else to the first principle of self, it can justify any behaviour, however antisocial. It is the vice that, more than any other, threatens social integrity.

Coriolanus is not timid about expressing pride. When his mother, wife and son come to plead for Rome he says:

> I'll never
> Be such a gosling to obey instinct, but stand
> As if a man were author of himself
> And knew no other kin. (V.iii.34–7)

He has made himself by himself, and therefore owes nothing and nobody – like Edmund's more attractive 'I should have been that I am had the maidenliest star in the firmament twinkled on my bastardizing' (I.ii.128–30). Coriolanus would be all things himself, as Sicinius, no less shrewd a judge of character for being himself corrupt, says:

> Where is this viper
> That would depopulate the city and
> Be every man himself? (III.i.261–3)

The central instance of Coriolanus's pride and the turning point of the plot occur simultaneously in a single event. The tribunes have cunningly engineered his banishment. After an ineffective attempt to appeal against the sentence by Cominius, it is restated by Brutus,

> There's no more to be said but he is banish'd,
> As enemy to the people and his country.
> It shall be so!

and it is echoed by the plebians:

> It shall be so, it shall be so! (III.iii.117–19).

Coriolanus immediately replies to his banishment by 'banishing' Rome:

> You common cry of curs! whose breath I hate
> As reek o'th'rotten fens, whose loves I prize
> As the dead carcasses of unburied men
> That do corrupt my air: I banish you! (III.iii.120–3)

This is an amazing solipsism – an individual cannot banish a state. Alcibiades in *Timon*, a parallel instance of state ingratitude to a military hero, who is banished for pleading mercy for a

comrade who has violated the law, responds with hostility like
Coriolanus but also with understanding:

> Banish me?
> Banish your dotage, banish usury,
> That makes the Senate ugly! (III.v.98–100)

Coriolanus is not quibbling over grammar and definition – his
outlook equates the individual Coriolanus with the state of
Rome. Donne, it is true, says he could 'eclipse' the sun by winking
(in 'The Sun Rising', *The Complete English Poems*, ed. A. J. Smith,
1978: Penguin, Harmondsworth), but that is clearly an exercise
of heroic wit; Coriolanus cannot recognise the difference and
seriously sees himself as an individual equal to the collective.

Coriolanus's attitude may be pathological but it is not in
opposition to, rather it is an exaggeration of, those of his fellow
patricians. Menenius, when he concludes the message of the belly
fable, summarises the position of the insurrection of the plebeians:
'Rome and her rats are at the point of battle' (I.i.161). Is Rome
only the patricians? Are those he calls rats not Romans? It is the
construction of this type of class division – between valid, true
members of the state and the unworthy poor, the riff-raff there by
accident – that provides the basis for Coriolanus's position. His
attitude is only an extreme form of that of Menenius.

Such class hostility, reinforced by his pride, makes it impossible
for Coriolanus to feel any kinship, positive relationship or
mutuality with the plebians. The Consul election ritual of
begging their voices is not, then, the celebration of a relationship
of service (the display of scars gained on their behalf) but an
unnecessary humiliation (revealing *his* wounds to the unworthy).
Thus he can say 'Better it is to die, better to starve,/ Than crave the
hire which first we do deserve' (II.iii.112–13). His desert is
independent of service for them, he would have that clear:

> To brag unto them, thus I did, and thus,
> Show them th'unaching scars which I should hide,
> As if I had receiv'd them for the hire
> Of their breath only! (II.ii.147–50)

This attitude does not pass without Roman criticism. When
Coriolanus refuses the offer made by the General, Cominius, of a
tenth of the plunder before general distribution, and also objects

to the ovation the Romans give him – 'acclamations hyperbolical,/ As if I lov'd my little should be dieted/ In praises sauc'd with lies' (I.ix.50–2) – Cominius replies:

> Too modest are you,
> More cruel to your good report than grateful
> To us that give you truly. (I.ix.52–4)

Cominius's remarks suggest an idea of public service that is mutual but Coriolanus cannot comprehend that service need not be mercenary; for him, pursuit of honour excludes any relation to the plebians. The Third Citizen answers Coriolanus's objection to begging from the plebians: 'You must think, if we give you anything, we hope to gain by you.' When Coriolanus then says, 'Well then, I pray, your price o'th'consulship?', the first Citizen answers: 'The price is, to ask it kindly' (II.iii.70–5). It is not merely courtesy that is demanded here; like the 'milk of human kindness' which Lady Macbeth scorns in her husband, it is recognition of social integrity. Coriolanus side-steps the issue saying (mockingly in word, if not in tone), 'Kindly, sir, I pray let me ha't' (II.iii.76). His hostility to the plebians is at one with his inability to see any social connection between himself and them.

The excessive military violence Coriolanus displays is made possible by his not recognising a connection between himself and the rest of mankind. This has been encouraged by the training he has received from his mother, who is clear that gaining honour in battle is the highest human activity. Whereas Coriolanus's wife Virgilia considers warfare from the standpoint of everyday living, Volumnia views ordinary life from the perspective of war:

> I, considering how honour would become such a person – that it was no better than picture-like to hang by th'wall, if renown made it not stir – was pleased to let him seek danger where he was like to find fame. (I.iii.9–14)

Death in battle is the culmination of life; had she a dozen sons, Volumnia says, 'I had rather had eleven die nobly for their country, than one voluptuously surfeit out of action' (I.iii.24–5). The warlike activity in which he engages is given concrete realisation by Shakespeare. It is more than Macbeth's heroic encounters – it is an elevation of warfare into pure destruction and quintessential aggression. Even Cominius, an older, more socialised patrician, praises Coriolanus in terms that must alienate the audience, going beyond the image of a human-engaged-in-violence to depict him as a force of inhuman destruction:

> from face to foot
> He was a thing of blood, whose every motion
> Was tim'd with dying cries (II.ii.108–10)

and his action is to

> Run reeking o'er the lives of men, as if
> 'Twere a perpetual spoil. (II.ii.119–20)

This is not noble encounter; it is heartless, mindless destruction, a violence that exceeds its purpose to such an extent that the means becomes an end in itself. When Coriolanus leads the Volscians against Rome, Cominius, who has previously praised his unstoppable destruction, recognises the same quality and says,

> they follow him
> Against us brats, with no less confidence
> Than boys pursuing summer butterflies,
> Or butchers killing flies. (IV.vi.93–6)

The final line characterises the value of human life. What a falling off from Hamlet's 'what piece of work is a man'.

Although the violence in the play may perhaps be given acceptance today on the false basis that it was regarded as necessary if not actually commendable in the culture of the time, it should be remembered that the Elizabethan–Jacobean age offers other images that are less accepting of immoderate violence and are not convinced of any necessary relation between wounds and valour. Thomas Nashe, in *The Unfortunate Traveller*, describes reactions to the slaughter of the Anabaptist followers of John Leiden:

> Pitiful and lamentable was their unpitied and well-performed slaughter. To see even a bear, which is the most cruellest of all beasts, too too bloodily overmatched and deformedly rent in pieces by an unconscionable number of curs, it would move compassion against kind, and make those that, beholding him at the stake yet uncoped with, wished him a suitable death to his ugly shape, now to re-call their hard-hearted wishes and moan him suffering as a mild beast, in

comparison of the foul-mouthed mastiffs, his butchers. Even such [compassion] did those overmatched ungracious Münsterians obtain of many indifferent eyes, who now thought them, suffering, to be sheep brought innocent to the shambles, whenas before they deemed them as a number of wolves up in arms against the shepherds. (Penguin ed., p.285)

Nashe is disgusted by senseless violence. Even in *Tamburlaine*, the play which probably has as violent a spirit as anything else in the age, Zenocrate says to Tamburlaine before he fights Bajazeth:

> And may my love, the King of Persia,
> Return with victory and free from wound!
>   (III.iii.132–3)

Shakespeare also casts doubt on the virtue in Coriolanus's violence insofar as it makes him a brute. He is a fighting machine, rather than a leader of men. Coriolanus is praised by Lartius for fulfilling Cato's ideal image of a soldier:

>   not fierce and terrible
> Only in strokes, but with thy grim looks and
> The thunder-like percussion of thy sounds. (I.iv.57–9)

This is like the use of the belly fable as a model for the body politic, reducing the body to its most animal, not human level; i.e., where we might expect the ideal of the soldier to include something humane, such as planning or tactics, we are given a reiteration of the 'thing of blood', pure violent physicality. Coriolanus is the fighter who foolishly enters the gates of the enemy all alone. This is not heroic Talbot, not brilliant Henry V, not cunning Achilles, but more beast than man. And so completely has the violence filled his consciousness that he transforms even situations of politics into physical military encounter – as when he would resist the aediles by force: 'Stand fast./ We have as many friends as enemies.' Menenius responds: 'Shall it be put to that?' and the First Senator says, 'The gods forbid' (III.i.229–31). Even for his own class, in the terms of their interests, Coriolanus's propensity for violence is inappropriate.

It should also be noted that, as well as casting doubts on brutish violence, the play includes some comic populist critique of war itself. Aufidius's servants, after the fashion of populist proverbial wit in praising the contrary position, offer ironic argument in favour of war: 'This peace is nothing but to rust iron, increase tailors, and breed ballad-makers . . . and as wars, in some sort, may be said to be a ravisher, so it cannot be denied but peace is a great maker of cuckolds . . . The wars for my money' (IV.v.226–38).

Shakespeare makes it obvious that Coriolanus's range of response is very limited, but that does not resolve the question of whether this limited behaviour is to be understood as vice or Roman virtue; i.e., is he a pathological killer or a man of integrity? Such stark contrasts are reductive and do violence to the play; either/or oppositions do not provide the material for tragedy. The problem Shakespeare confronts is one of balance and the transformation of qualities, where, for example, the 'good' qualities function contrary to the way they should, where virtue turns into vice or vice acquires characteristics of virtue.

Coriolanus, in the words of Menenius, is of such composition that:

> His nature is too noble for the world:
> He would not flatter Neptune for his trident,
> Or Jove for's power to thunder. His heart's his mouth:
> What his breast forges, that his tongue must vent.
>   (III.i.253–6)

This is noble and attractive, open, direct, free of the calculation and subterfuge of the politicians (especially those like Brutus and Sicinius). It is steadfast, in contrast to the fickleness of the populace who accept Coriolanus for Consul, then reject and banish him, and then claim they banished him 'unwillingly': 'I ever said we were i'th'wrong when we banished him', says the First Citizen, and the Second Citizen replies, 'So did we all' (IV.vi.155–7). This dishonesty and rationalisation do not touch Coriolanus. He stands like a rock, pounded by the sea, unmoving, unmoved, remaining himself. Yet Volumnia qualifies this:

>   You are too absolute.
> Though therein you can never be too noble,
> But when extremities speak. (III.ii.39–41)

That is, his nobility, unbending, is unsuited for moments of political crisis; nobility, in general the highest behaviour, must yield to *other* considerations in political life, or it becomes its opposite, furthering the ignoble (this is reminiscent of the problem of Macbeth's 'Vaulting ambition, which o'erleaps itself/ And falls on th'other' – I.vii.27–8). In isolation the integrity is a virtue; in context it is destructive, of self and others. The remarks of the Officers, in an interchange serving no purpose other than commentary, contextualises his actions in a neutral, choric manner. The First Officer mentions Coriolanus's pride and dislike of the common people. The Second Officer elaborates on this, saying Coriolanus's indifference to the affections of the populace is noble: 'out of his noble carelessness lets them plainly see't' (II.ii.14–15). Coriolanus actively seeks their hatred, says the first Officer, and 'to affect the malice and displeasure of the people is as bad as that which he dislikes, to flatter them for their love' (II.ii.21–3). The behaviour is self-indulgent. The other face of 'integrity' is solipsism.

Whether one chooses to regard it positively or not, in his 'integrity' Coriolanus suffers from a reduced humanity. Macbeth and Antony have a richness of imagination inaccessible to him. Coriolanus is no more than an iron man, 'he moves like an engine', as Menenius says (V.iv.18–19). The most telling picture is that of the father reflected in the son. In his behaviour young Martius is seen as the image of his father by both Volumnia and Valeria, a noble friend, who elaborates her praise:

> I looked upon him o' Wednesday half an hour together: 'has such a confirmed countenance. I saw him run after a gilded butterfly, and when he caught it, he let it go again, and after it again, and over and over he comes, and up again, catched it again; or whether his fall enraged him, or how 'twas, he did so set his teeth and tear it. Oh, I warrant how he mammocked it! (I.iii.58–65)

Given the attention Shakespeare pays elsewhere, as in the Sonnets, to the exquisite delicacy of the butterfly, this encounter between fragile beauty and brute force cannot be understood as anything but monstrous. The choice of a butterfly as the object of this mindless violence removes all doubt that it has a negative value. There is no place in the world of Coriolanus for delicacy, colour, reflection, softness, hesitancy, creativity, warmth; social feeling is gone. If we accept the cliche from Donne's Meditation XVII that says, 'no man is an island' (from *Devotions upon Emergent Occasions*, 1986, University of Michigan Press, Ann Arbor, p. 108), we can recognise as a corollary that an isolated figure like Coriolanus cannot be a man, except in the most limited biological sense, 'a poor, bare, forked animal' (*King Lear*, III.iv.105–6). Menenius sees, finally, the monster in the man:

> There is differency between a grub and a butterfly; yet your butterfly was a grub. This Martius is grown from man to dragon.
> (V.iv.11–13)

Coriolanus is recognised as a psychopath who thinks he is a hero. Albany, reflecting on Goneril's behaviour, says,

> She that herself will sliver and disbranch
> From her material sap, perforce must wither
> And come to deadly use. (IV.ii.34–6)

Coriolanus, in severing himself from Rome, engineers his own downfall, as Aufidius observes:

> When Caius, Rome is thine,
> Thou art poor'st of all: then shortly art thou mine.
> (IV.vii.56–7)

When Volumnia tells him he can have no honour in slaughtering Rome the contradiction between vengeance and honour is too great – he breaks. Aufidius says, aside,

> I am glad thou hast set thy mercy and thy honour
> At difference in thee. Out of that I'll work
> Myself a former fortune. (V.iii.200–2)

Coriolanus, alone, is humiliated and killed by Aufidius; alone, he is nothing. In the balance of society and self, by becoming all self he became no self. Thinking his honour was his own, instead of a relation between people, he destroyed his honour.

Timon of Athens

In *Timon of Athens* Shakespeare reaches the logical limit of social disintegration – a 'society' of atomistic individuals whose most basic social attributes have undergone an asocial transformation – and it would seem he has also exhausted the larger images – the 'action' of Aristotle – that can convey dramatically the significance of that transformation. The play suffers from too much telling instead of showing, and the action sometimes needs interpretation by outside commentary, as when the First Stranger characterises the refusal of his 'friends' to aid Timon:

> But I perceive
> Men must learn now with pity to dispense,
> For policy sits above conscience. (III.ii.87–9)

Sometimes the emotional significance is underscored verbally in speech directed more toward the audience than to other characters, as when Timon's servant Flaminius, also failing to secure aid for Timon, says:

> Is't possible the world should so much differ,
> And we alive that lived? (III.i.46–7)

Much of what is 'showing' has a formal character, rhetorically balanced illustrations of a point, that make it seem more like telling. The philosophical/moral discussions on stage are often the primary material to which the audience must attend – what the play is *about*. This is quite different from discourse where the importance lies in another context, for example, the dialogue between Osric and Hamlet, where the literal burden of the discourse is irrelevant and the point is the hollowness, affectation and lack of integrity of the Court.

Timon relies on stylised, formally balanced incidents – emblem-like scenes such as Shakespeare used in the *Henry VI* plays – with no concentration of individualising detail. It moves from the extended discourse at the opening, through examples of Timon giving, counterbalanced then by examples of Timon failing to get money back, to emblematic scenes of Timon as a hermit. His banquets, major focuses of the plot, serve the same function *analytically* as the banquet in *Macbeth*, but they do not

have the development of concrete experience that can produce
feeling-understanding rather than just rational comprehension.
Like Apemantus's aphoristic wisdom, which closes instead of
opening questions, the result is the reduction of complex characteristics to label-like qualities. Thus Timon is identified as
prominent, noble, and above all generous – but these are
different from qualities understood through interchange and
action, such as the integrity-as-pride or pride-as-integrity of
Coriolanus. Nevertheless the play carries further the picture of
social decline. This is not presented primarily in the ill-treatment
Timon receives at the hands of his former 'friends' – ingratitude
'worse than stealth' (III.iv.28) as one of their servants puts it –
but in the character of Timon's own attitudes. As in *Coriolanus*,
the concern is the private appropriation of a social relationship.
Where Coriolanus could serve as an instance of social disintegration in treating honour as a private possession rather than a
relationship, Timon fulfils the same function by failing to understand that generosity, too, is a relationship between people, not a
quality 'possessed' by an individual. *Timon* is a decline from
Coriolanus because generosity is the most fundamental of social
qualities – the sense of the genus, recognition of one's kind and
consequent sense of kinship. Timon's mistaken generosity is
made worse by having a clear instrument, gold, the means
through which social relations can be privately controlled.

Timon's bounty knows no limits but, unlike Antony's which
was poetically given humane qualities – an autumn harvest that
had 'no winter in't' (V.ii.87), Timon understands only quantity.
In the words of the Second Lord:

> He pours it out. Plutus the god of gold
> Is but his steward. No meed but he repays
> Seven-fold above itself: no gift to him
> But breeds the giver a return exceeding
> All use of quittance. (I.i.275–9)

The excess destroys its character of generosity – which would be
a response appropriate to the situation – and it is recognised as
ridiculous by one of the Senators:

> If I want gold, steal but a beggar's dog
> And give it Timon – why, the dog coins gold;

If I would sell my horse and buy twenty moe
Better than he – why, give my horse to Timon;
Ask nothing, give it him, it foals me straight
And able horses. (II.i.5–10)

Whatever the indications to the contrary, Timon chooses to see this giving as a relationship. When he gives his servant Lucilius money equal to the dowry of the women he courts, he says,

To build his fortune I will strain a little,
For 'tis a bond in men. (I.i.146–7)

When Apemantus objects to the constant riot of luxury, 'What needs these feasts, pomps, and vain-glories?', Timon responds: 'Nay, and you begin to rail on society once, I am sworn not to give regard to you' (I.ii.244,245–6); he is trying to see his acts as social. He asserts the social character of the banquet, telling the assembled Lords that ceremony was designed

To set a gloss on faint deeds . . .
But where there is true friendship, there needs none.
Pray, sit; more welcome are ye to my fortunes
Than my fortunes to me. (I.ii.16–20)

The First Lord is quite willing to echo conventionally the suggestion of mutuality, making a plea to Timon: 'that you would once use our hearts' (I.ii.83), and Timon accepts that this is an accurate reflection of the relation between them. When the steward weeps, seeing only disaster in Timon's finances, Timon says, 'Why dost thou weep? Canst thou the conscience lack,/ To think I shall lack friends? Secure thy heart' (II.ii.179–80). And when the senators have refused to help Timon he tells the steward 'look cheerly', and attributes the lack of assistance to old age affecting the senators: ''Tis lack of kindly warmth they are not kind' (II.ii.218,221).

The role of Apemantus as someone explicitly antisocial makes it easier for Timon to appear the opposite; i.e., Apemantus, in rejecting Timon's behaviour, would seem to confirm him as social. Thus 'Apemantus' Grace':

Immortal gods, I crave no pelf;
I pray for no man but myself.
Grant I may never prove so fond,
To trust man on his oath or bond;
Or a harlot for her weeping,
Or a dog that seems a-sleeping,
Or a keeper with my freedom,
Or my friends, if I should need 'em.
Amen. So fall to 't:
Rich men sin, and I eat root. (I.ii.62–71)

Besides the doubt Shakespeare casts on Timon's generosity by other characters' observation of his heedless giving, the phrasing of remarks by the servants, the only positive characters in the play, puts in question the relationship Timon has supposedly created on the basis of his gifts. The Steward says:

Heavens, have I said, the bounty of this lord!
How many prodigal bits have slaves and peasants
This night englutted! Who is not Timon's?
What heart, head, sword, force, means, but is Lord Timon's,
Great Timon, noble, worthy, royal Timon?
Ah, when the means are gone that buy this praise,
The breath is gone whereof this praise is made.
Feast-won, fast-lost; one cloud of winter show'rs,
These flies are couch'd. (II.ii.168–76)

More than making explicit that the relationship depends on Timon's continuous giving, the statement suggests in the phrase 'who is not Timon's' that what exists is something different from a mutual relationship. They are not 'Timon's *friends*' but simply 'Timon's'; the relationship is dependence, even ownership.

The general character in which these specific relationships exist is expressed in discussion of the power of gold. The Poet, for example, explains this to the Painter:

You see how all conditions, how all minds,
As well of glib and slipp'ry creatures as
Of grave and austere quality, tender down
Their services to Lord Timon: his large fortune,
Upon his good and gracious nature hanging,
Subdues and properties to his love and tendance
All sorts of hearts; yea, from the glass-fac'd flatterer

To Apemantus, that few things loves better
Than to abhor himself – even he drops down
The knee before him, and returns in peace
Most rich in Timon's nod. (I.i.53–63)

In the Poet's image it is Fortune 'Whose present grace to present
slaves and servants/ Translates his rivals' (I.i.73–4) so that (with
an image that must have struck Webster forcibly, being so similar
to Flamineo's complaint in *The White Devil*):

All those which were his fellows but of late,
Some better than his value . . .
Make sacred even his stirrup. (I.i.80–4)

Finally, Shakespeare gives Timon a set speech on the power of
gold (which, probably more than anything else in the play, has
entered popular consciousness):

What is here?
Gold? Yellow, glittering, precious gold?
No, gods, I am no idle votarist.
Roots, you clear heavens! Thus much of this will make
Black, white; foul, fair; wrong, right;
Base, noble; old, young; coward, valiant.
Ha, you gods! Why this? What this, you gods? Why, this
Will lug your priests and servants from your sides,
Pluck stout men's pillows from below their heads.
This yellow slave
Will knit and break religions, bless th'accurs'd,
Make the hoar leprosy ador'd, place thieves,
And give them title, knee and approbation
With senators on the bench. This is it
That makes the wappen'd widow wed again:
She whom the spital-house and ulcerous sores
Would cast the gorge at, this embalms and spices
To th'April day again. Come, damn'd earth,
Thou common whore of mankind, that puts odds
Among the rout of nations, I will make thee
Do thy right nature. (IV.iii.25–45)

Timon repeats the ideas, with different instances of the same
transforming quality, some 350 lines later.

Although Shakespeare may have made Timon's intensity of
rage unique among discussions of gold's transforming power, the

theme had a continuous presence at least since Rabelais's *Gargan-
tua and Pantagruel* and Cornelius Agrippa's *Vanity and
Uncertainty of Arts and Sciences*. A speech of striking similarity
opens the almost exactly contemporary *Volpone*:

> Riches, the dumb god that giv'st all men tongues,
> That canst do nought, and yet mak'st men do all things;
> The price of souls; even hell, with thee to boot,
> Is made worth heaven! Thou art virtue, fame,
> Honour, and all things else. Who can get thee,
> He shall be noble, valiant, honest, wise.
>   (Penguin edition, I.i.22–7)

The same concept is in effect enacted in *The Alchemist* a few years
later.

Timon is reduced to nothing when the gold runs out. There
were no relationships to sustain him, for his generosity had been
entirely his own quality, like a possession. Like his tragic
predecessors, whose individualism mocked social relations –
Coriolanus, Macbeth, even Lear and Gloucester to an extent –
his unwillingness to face concrete relations with others leaves him
alone. The problem was not the lack of moderation pointed out
by Apemantus ('The middle of humanity thou never knewest,
but the extremity of both ends' – IV.iii.301–2) but, as with
Coriolanus, the pride, the understanding of generosity that failed
to recognise its character as a social relationship. This is articulated by the faithful steward, who concludes:

> Who would be so mock'd with glory, or to live
> But in a dream of friendship,
> To have his pomp and all what state compounds
> But only painted like his varnish'd friends? (IV.ii.33–6)

The steward's sense of Timon's failure echoes Macbeth's recognition that he has failed to gain the honour, love, friends, he
sought, that his life had 'fall'n into the sere, the yellow leaf'
(V.iii.23).

Timon invites his false friends to a final feast – the image of
true sociability – but it is a mock feast, appropriate to hollow
friendship, where the 'food' is revealed to be only smoke and
lukewarm water. Preceding the 'meal' Timon says a suitable
grace. This is not merely raillery, in the manner of Apemantus,

but a characterisation of the world in which he moves, which
Timon has now learned by experience:

> You great benefactors, sprinkle our society with thankfulness. For
> your own gifts, make yourselves prais'd; but reserve still to give, lest
> your deities be despis'd. Lend to each man enough, that one need not
> lend to another; for were your godheads to borrow of men, men
> would forsake the gods. Make the meat be belov'd, more than the
> man that gives it. Let no assembly of twenty be without a score of
> villains. If there sit twelve women at the table, let a dozen of them be
> as they are. The rest of your fees, O gods, the Senators of Athens,
> together with the common leg of people – what is amiss in them,
> you gods, make suitable for destruction. For these my present
> friends, as they are to me nothing, so in nothing bless them, and to
> nothing are they welcome. (III.vi.69–81)

Timon's 'nothing' becomes substantial; it is the thing his guests
are offered and what they are to be blessed in. This is different
from Cordelia's 'nothing', which is a true negative. Timon is not
saying anything logically different from Lear's 'nothing will come
of nothing' but the perspective is different. Lear speaks from a
sense of 'something', a condition not being fulfilled, whereas
Timon's bitterness expects nothing, 'nothing' is the content of his
expectation.

The guests at the feast are without embarrassment – their
comments on being driven out are uncomprehending and suggest only that they think Timon mad: 'One day he gives us
diamonds, next day stones' (III.vi.115). This is paralleled by their
inability to make any judgement of his actions, as when the First
Lord replies to the Second Lord's description of Timon's unbal-
anced giving, missing the point and saying, 'The noblest mind he
carries/ That ever govern'd man' (I.i.279–80). The forms no
longer have a content – they are the contrary of what Apemantus
called the 'extremity' of humanity, *mere* forms to which people
are indifferent. The scene is reminiscent of *Hamlet*, where the
hero's rage is met with incomprehension and indifference.

Shakespeare's presentation of the response of the guests
changes the emphasis from the hero to the world in which he
moves. In effect Shakespeare had already moved the play from
Timon to the world by presenting the banishment of Alcibiades
in the scene which precedes the mock banquet. The Senators who

banish him are shown to be corrupt, not unlike *Coriolanus*'s
Sicinius and Brutus, and Alcibiades directs his anger in a more
appropriate way than Coriolanus. His vision has not lost its social
quality, but to be social, in this world, is to be mad:

> I'm worse than mad: I have kept back their foes,
> While they have told their money, and let out
> Their coin upon large interest; I myself
> Rich only in large hurts. All those, for this?
>   (III.v.107–10)

Shakespeare's emphasis when Timon turns against Athens is
on 'kind', which is only a different angle of approach to social
being. The word occurs reasonably frequently since *As You Like
It* and has been significant since Hamlet's cliche about Claudius
– 'A little more than kin, and less than kind' (I.ii.65). The
question that hangs on the word, as in Lady Macbeth's 'milk of
human kindness', is what is human.

Timon characterises society in his extended malediction on
Athens. Like Lear cursing Goneril, Timon asks for various evils
to be visited on Athens, but these appear to be only an extension
of what already exists: for example,

>   Bound servants, steal!
> Large-handed robbers your grave masters are,
> And pill by law. Maid, to thy master's bed;
> Thy mistress is o'th'brothel! (IV.i.10–13)

His action that follows on the curse is to escape civilisation:

> Timon will to the woods, where he shall find
> Th'unkindest beast more kinder than mankind.
>   (IV.i.35–6)

The kindness here, like the plebians' price of consulship, 'to ask it
kindly', which Coriolanus is unable to understand, is only
secondarily 'benevolent', 'well-disposed', etc.; primarily it concerns the possession of social feeling. It involves recognising
kinship with other creatures of the same sort, with kind. It is
from acting on this sense of fellowship that 'kind' in the
secondary sense arises; it is fundamentally the same as 'generous',
which derives from 'genus' or kind. It was this that Timon lacked

– he failed, as it were, to grasp the genus in generosity – and it is the same quality that he painfully finds missing in society.

The atomisation of society is the counterpart of absence of kindness. When the bandits seeking gold from Timon say they cannot live like beasts, birds and fish on grass and berries, Timon's reply negates the possibility of kind:

> Nor on the beasts themselves, the birds and fishes;
> You must eat men. (IV.iii.427–8)

Albany's prophecy has been fulfilled – people have become monsters of the deep and devour each other. The progress, for Timon, is completed in the note on his tomb: 'Some beast read this; there does not live a man' (V.iii.4). 'Man' is more than the poor 'forked animal' only by virtue of society which, now disintegrated, leaves only beasts. When society perishes, humanity must perish. Recognition of kind, the ultimate human quality, has been destroyed. The realisation of the truth does not compensate for the loss; tragedy is no longer possible. Shakespeare turns to fantasy and romance.

CHAPTER VIII

Conclusion

When Hamlet said, 'What piece of work is a man, how noble in reason, how infinite in faculties' (II.ii.303–4), Shakespeare was referring to humankind, not isolated individuals. In the same way as people, animals, angels, all things in the late medieval view owed their excellence to being part of the Great Chain of Being, so Shakespeare was born into a world where the admirable qualities of people were seen as the result of participation in greater structures and interaction with others. To be civilised was equivalent to being humane; the contrary, being rude – unformed, inexperienced, ignorant – was to be merely the raw material, not the finished product, of humanity. Society, not biology, produced humanity. The wolf-reared child of the Middle Ages was a different creature, not *Homo sapiens* but *Homo ferus*, wild man.

Shakespeare explains the social nature of humanity most fully in *King Lear* (which is why that play can be regarded as his central work). At the same time he shows humane qualities to be rather perishable. The gap between ideal and real, between aspiration and actualisation, easily widens to a gulf. Like the laws of hospitality or filial piety, codes which result from custom rather than legislation, humane social relations work through mutuality and trust. They have no defensive mechanisms; they are subject to corruption and prey to selfish behaviour. Sometime in the mid-1590s Shakespeare's plays begin to show awareness of how relations based on trust were vulnerable to self-interested principles.

His first treatment of this conflict of custom and self-interest was *Richard II*. King Richard and Bolingbroke are more than two individuals in conflict; they are made to represent a struggle between hierarchical and individualist world-views. Although Richard violates accepted codes in seizing Bolingbroke's inheritance, he has authority as King to insist on Bolingbroke's banishment. And when Bolingbroke returns to England, contrary to the terms of his banishment, he claims he comes, not to challenge Richard's authority, but only to seek his own property, which Richard had wrongfully seized. The principle of the individual vanquishes the principle of hierarchy; the right of ownership defeats the right of authority.

The two sets of principles are incompatible: there is no way in which Bolingbroke's victory and his principle of ownership could be justified in the terms of the old inherited principles of the country. The justifications are expediency and self-interest, what is called 'commodity' in the contemporary *King John*. Because Bolingbroke as Henry IV reigns without the authority of the old principles and tradition, his rule must remain unsettled. The self-interest that justified his kingship could as easily justify rebellion. The country has been plagued with 'intestine shock/ And furious close of civil butchery' (1 *Henry IV*, I.i.12–13). This instability and disorder constitute the formal subject of the *Henry IV* plays, but, at a deeper level, they also characterise ordinary life.

The *Henry IV* plays deal with disorder in a way that is mostly humorous. Within a framework of ostensible order, royal purposes and the conduct of the state, there is an underworld in which the heart of the plays beats and which is more concretely realised than any of the royal scenes. The principles on which this underlife is conducted are not articulated directly; they are a transformation of the obsolescent high ideals of the society, a use of old terms with a new content. Falstaff is the genius of this revision of the relation between word and referent. He presents a charming image of his projected career as a highwayman:

> let us be Diana's foresters, gentlemen of the shade, minions of the moon; and let men say we be men of good government, being governed as the sea is, by our noble and chaste mistress the moon, under whose countenance we steal. (I.ii.25–9)

Here we have the engaging Vice, making the bad appear good through concealing its activity in gracious and courtly terms. This innocent fun becomes more pernicious when Falstaff begins to rob goodness of meaning and to make it thereby irrelevant, as when he says to Hal, 'I would to God thou and I knew where a commodity of good names were to be bought' (1 *Henry IV*, I.ii.80–1). The purchase of reputation is a commonplace of the age but Falstaff also undermines the concept of 'good name' by making it directly an object of purchase, a 'commodity'. As in his equation of pox and gout, he destroys standards.

Falstaff teaches this linguistic expediency to Hal. When Hal defends himself before his father, promising to conduct himself henceforth in a manner befitting a prince and to atone for his Cheapside habits, he offers a rich chivalric vision of overcoming Percy:

> For the time will come
> That I shall make this northern youth exchange
> His glorious deeds for my indignities.
> Percy is but my factor, good my lord,
> To engross up glorious deeds on my behalf,
> And I will call him to so strict account
> That he shall render every glory up,
> Yea, even the slightest worship of his time,
> Or I will tear the reckoning from his heart.
> (1 *Henry IV*, III.ii.144–52)

The vision, on closer examination, appears tainted: Percy has become a 'factor', a commercial agent, to 'engross' is to buy up all the commodity in a region to make it dearer, and 'account' and 'reckoning' are obviously related to business. The commercial terminology transforms the chivalric content: chivalry becomes no more than an image that no longer reflects the material reality. The content of the image, the reality, is business; the image mere advertising.

When Hal rejects Falstaff on becoming king in 2 *Henry IV*, this is required by the demands of royalty, but it can also be understood as the Prince's graduation from the school of Falstaff – he has learned all he needs to know about manipulation of image (as the scene of his rhetorical casting-off of Falstaff shows). In *Henry V* the young King manipulates an army with the skill he used to get round his father; his heroic performance is balanced by his self-interest and cynicism. The disorder of the *Henry IV* plays has been refined and become institutionalised –

as order – in *Henry V*. Juxtaposing the ideal and the reality, Shakespeare offers a critical view of public order without destroying the idea.

In the Second History Cycle delight in the wit of transformation outweighs the cynicism at the degeneration of standards. Falstaff and Prince Hal are genial, and the slippage of language is exuberant, funny and only potentially dangerous. The transfer of linguistic manipulation to the larger world of politics has a seriousness evaded in the earlier manifestations, and, as king, Hal offers as much threat as promise. The development passes a critical point after the Second History Cycle: in *Hamlet*, for the first time, the disintegration of the society becomes tragic. *Hamlet* anchors the floating cynicism of *Henry V* in concrete rage.

A pattern emerges in the tragedies from *Hamlet* to *Timon of Athens*. There is a developing clarity in Shakespeare's dramatisation of social argument, and there is a perception of the society in a process of change. It is needless to stress that this pattern is to be found not in the literal subjects – histories of heroic Romans or British kings – but in the metaphors, the imaginative (non-logical) relation these subjects have to the world the audience lived in. The metaphors are not logical abstractions fleshed out with neutral pieces of reality but the embodiment of responses to lived experience. The emotional attitudes to the historical reality of the audience gives them a power and shapes them. It is through the metaphors that the plays engage with reality. And the development of a pattern of those metaphors helps make clearer their significance.

The drawing of such a pattern would probably be meaningless for the contemporary audiences for the plays – they were living the experience evaluated in the plays – but for audiences and readers today a sense of the whole pattern can make each part clearer. An experience that is entirely new cannot be understood; novelty needs to be related to things already understood to be comprehensible. Shakespeare's plays were composed largely of material the contemporary audience already knew – vogue terms, current stereotypes, shared local experience of a changing world, etc. Out of the reorganisation of such experience, the plays could generate fresh understanding and alter attitudes.

The attitudes of the time are available for us mainly from the rest of the plays and other literary material of the day. But they can seldom be read off directly from the plays. The problem is less, say, 'did Shakespeare approve of Fortinbras?' than how and to what degree his approval is qualified. The significance of the plays lies not in bald facts but in the subtleties of their relation to other aspects of living. When Coriolanus says to the Romans, 'I banish you,' for example, is this Roman petulance or does it signify anything of importance to the audience? When Macbeth asks night to 'cancel and tear to pieces that great bond which keeps me pale', how drastic does the audience find destoying his 'bond'? When Timon holds a banquet, what social resonance does that have? These questions can all be answered, at least in part, from the plays in which they occur, but Shakespeare is building the plays out of materials, events and qualities, that have a social existence already for the audience. To be able to observe behaviour in a number of contexts makes it more comprehensible; and seeing a pattern of developing argument for the tragedies, as it were, contextualises the contexts.

The movement of the tragedies, from *Hamlet* to *Timon of Athens*, is not a change of kind – the subject they all treat is the rending of the social fabric – but one of degree. Hamlet's melancholy, his rage and sometimes overwhelming sense of depression, are his response to the complacency of the world of Elsinore. Timon's all-consuming hatred, in the final tragedy, is a response to an almost unrelieved, totally irresponsible pursuit of wealth. The social integrity of the playworlds deteriorates from play to play.

Hamlet rages that Elsinore scorns the decency and integrity he has been led to believe in – things are supposed to be a certain way, but that is not how they are. The disparity is produced out of self-seeking. Rules have been broken, trust shattered, humanity betrayed. The rage gains its force from the sense of Elizabethan social decline, the deterioration of standards, that was much discussed at the time. The decline pictured in the playworld of *Hamlet* is visible to the contemporary audience outside the theatre as well as in the play itself.

There is also in *Hamlet* a feeling of loss. The excellent image of human dignity expressed in the Great Chain of Being seems to be false. Man gained dignity by being placed directly below the angels in the Chain, 'in apprehension how like a god' as Hamlet said, but that vision must be abandoned. Hamlet has to judge by what he sees before him and concludes: 'what is this quintessence of dust?' (II.ii.306, 308). There is all the pain of adolescent disillusionment at a world gone bad.

Yet the play shows to some extent a positive attitude on the part of Shakespeare because it assumes that Hamlet's rage will be comprehensible to the audience, that there is enough of a community of values remaining that the subject of his rage will be recognised and responded to with sympathy.

In *King Lear* Shakespeare felt it necessary to explain, with concrete instances, why the changes that society was undergoing were damaging. There is no dispute as to the facts of the case, as it were; there is agreement that a certain type of behaviour is common in the society. The question then relates to what is wrong with it. Is it a case of Gertrude saying 'I doubt it is no other but the main' (II.ii.56)? Thus *King Lear* does not rely on definitions – the terms are not the subject of any disagreement – but demonstrates the significance of certain positions through their consequences in action for people's lives. It *shows* the results of the new logic. The drama, as I have argued in the second chapter on *Lear*, objectifies.

Even if people are unwilling to approve of throwing old men into the storm or putting out their eyes, they may follow the same principles that ultimately justify such behaviour. To show the consequences of principles in *King Lear* constitutes a forceful social critique but it can still be seen as positive in that Shakespeare appears confident that audience recognition of the objective consequences provides sufficient grounds for rejecting the principle. Although the prospect offered for society at the end of the play is none too bright, the action has succeeded in conveying a powerful sense of what is important in life and what it means to be human.

Macbeth illustrates a further decline because there is a confusion of social and individualistic logic – the ethical base from which the play starts is lower. The effects on individuals are demonstrated in a way that makes the problem much more personal, the consequences more particular. Shakespeare shows how individualistic logic destroys, for individuals as well as for society, the very things it is invoked to achieve. Less hopeful in final prospect than *King Lear*, with the one bearer of social awareness dead, the play still has a positive aspect. The very energy of the art involved in the brilliant union of form and content is itself optimistic, and there is again something hopeful in the clarity of its understanding. It moves from *Lear*'s documentary horror to the sense of someone 'like ourselves' of traditional tragedy, which allows the play to be felt in a way more personal than *Lear*. It is understandable as a personal example rather than an object lesson.

In *Antony and Cleopatra* socially orientated behaviour has practically disappeared but still exists as a warm memory. Antony cannot rise above the degradation of Rome, but his aspiration to do so is still attractive, suggesting a richer notion of humanity and showing with inescapable clarity the oppressive nature of Rome – its idea of virtue that negates what is humane and what gives richness to life. It is nostalgic, harking back to when things were different; it is 'the twilight of such day/ As after sunset fadeth in the west' (Sonnet 73), the twilight of the old world.

In *Coriolanus* only the image of a social integrity remains, because it is necessary to justify the power relations. Social qualities are not recognised (as they were in *Antony and Cleopatra*, even if not regarded), and there is nothing to relieve the hostility. There are no groups that receive approval, and if the plebians are presented as having reasonable cause for complaint, they are not made any more attractive for that. And even the usual source of hope, children, turns repulsive in the play.

In *Timon of Athens*, finally, the sense of what is the norm has obviously changed. Athens is an atomistic society of intensely self-seeking individuals, where, with the exception of the servants, there is nothing but a collection of empty social forms, a cloak that covers naked self-interest without concealing it, easily discarded when Timon becomes hostile. Tragedy necessarily relies on social material – without any recognition of social bond we have case studies instead of tragedy. In *Timon* the social element is reduced so near to nothing that, in effect, the subject of tragedy disappears. The social longing that gave resonance to the poetry of *Macbeth* is blighted; the verse of *Timon* is larger than its literal content and resonates only in its expression of hostility, in Timon's hatred of gold. The decline of society has gone too far to generate any positive attitude.

Timon of Athens was the end of Shakespeare's career as a tragedian. He turned next to romances, plays that strain naturalism with artifice, that are brilliant exercises of technique, but which avoid structures that can have more than a passing reference to the real world. The society imagined in earlier tragedies was dead; perhaps it was no longer worth facing reality.

APPENDIX

Othello and tragedy

Othello differs from the rest of Shakespeare's tragedies in being constructed in a way that avoids the essential principles of tragedy common to the others. The chief of these is *necessity*. It is not a principle that precedes the play but something that, empirically, is connected with the way that tragedies function. It involves a process of events from which the conclusion is perceived to result necessarily — as opposed to casually or accidentally — from the conditions that preceded it. These conditions need not be impersonal: one of the elements of necessity is usually what in Aristotle's *Poetics* is called 'character'. This is not personality but what a person will or will not choose to do in circumstances where the choice is not obvious — i.e., it is essentially a person's principles.

The way necessity works can be seen clearly in *Hamlet*. The audience soon knows that Hamlet must eventually meet a disaster, *necessarily*, because there is a fundamental contradiction between the menacing self-interest of the Court at Elsinore and the hero's concern with decency and uprightness. It is clear that Elsinore is not going to mend its ways and that Hamlet is not going to lose his integrity, which puts them on an inevitable collision course. In this sense the disaster is built into the material of the play. The course the action is going to take is perceived before it happens (we anticipate Hamlet's death) and is unattractive and disturbing to contemplate. At this point, when it is recognised where things will lead, experiential response and analytic response diverge. In *Hamlet*, at the experiential level, the audience is concerned for Hamlet: is there any way he can avoid disaster? Should he, say, go back to Wittenberg? That would probably remove him from Claudius's murderous attention, but

it would also mean giving up the fight, acceding to the corruption at Elsinore, and thereby giving up the basis of audience
affection for him. Could we accept a Hamlet who pursued an
easy life? There is no solution that will preserve both Hamlet's life
and our admiration for him: we must accept that the disaster is
inevitable.

The end result of this acceptance of necessity is the catharsis
that Aristotle identifies as the goal of tragedy. In recognising that
what we do not want to happen *must* happen, we accept the
disagreeable in anticipation. The movement of the action towards
the disaster is fraught with the tension between aversion and
recognition of necessity. The completion of the action, the
disaster itself, resolves that tension. In that sense the completion
of the process is *formally* pleasurable, even though its content is
unpleasant. What 'had to be' has been; there is the release of it
being over.

This release can occur *only* if the process leading to the disaster
is felt to be necessary. If it did not 'have to be', the result is
accidental – it *could* have been another way – and is therefore
unpleasant without having anything that makes it acceptable.
There is no convincing answer to the question 'why?'; it nags at
the mind, ever unsatisfactory. Apart from *Othello*, all the tragedies
discussed in this study have, with varying degrees of clearness,
dramatic necessity (*King Lear* works in a somewhat different way
because the character function is transferred from the individual
to social type and the will of a single individual has less effect in
determining the outcome than in any other of the tragedies).

Only at the most general level did the disaster of *Othello* 'have
to be'; in terms of plot, at the level of specific detail, it was more
casual than necessary. The heroes move in an environment that
opposes their goodness, and in that sense they are bound to fail.
Against Venice's commercial (and insofar as Iago is a bearer of
Venetian culture, materialistic) background, Othello and Desdemona present an idealised excellence. Both are great-hearted souls
who rise above the petty concerns of material life. They marry
against convention, without calculation of advantage, on the
basis of a love founded on mutual recognition of their characters.
Thus Othello tells the Senate that Desdemona said, 'she wish'd/
That heaven had made her such a man' (I.iii.162–3) and she in

effect proposed to him. Othello's magnanimity is displayed in his
rhetoric. When Brabantio seeks out Othello, hoping to stop his
daughter's elopement, and the men of the two sides draw their
weapons, Othello says:

> Keep up your bright swords, for the dew will rust 'em;
> Good signior, you shall more command with years
> Than with your weapons. (I.ii.59–61)

He rises magnificently above common anger, and at the same
time displays a socialised regard for age. Desdemona, expressing
the heroic dignity of the individual, is a perfect counterpart.
When she badgers Othello about meeting Cassio to reconsider
the latter's disgrace, Othello at length replies: 'Prithee no
more, let him come when he will,/ I will deny thee nothing'
(III.iii.76–7). Her immediate response is to articulate the difference between asking that he do something sensible and asking
that he do something because he loves her:

> Why, this is not a boon,
> 'Tis as I should entreat you wear your gloves;
> Or feed on nourishing dishes, or keep you warm,
> Or sue to you, to do a peculiar profit
> To your own person: nay, when I have a suit
> Wherein I mean to touch your love indeed,
> It shall be full of poise and difficulty,
> And fearful to be granted. (III.iii.77–84)

Othello and Desdemona are not 'too good to be true' but too
good to last. They do not present an idealism such as that
manifested by Hamlet from time to time, a noble view of
mankind which is not evident in the reality immediately before
him ('What piece of work is a man, how noble in reason, how
infinite in faculties . . . in action how like an angel, in apprehension how like a god' – II.ii.303–6). Rather they are idealists
in the sense of refusing to recognise actualities. Thus Desdemona
can give as good as she gets when Iago utters his traditional
misogynist view of women, part of his general negative view of
humanity that he would pass off as realism, but she is also willing
to insist on a conventionally ideal image of women in her
dialogue with the humane and realistic Emilia about adultery:

Des.	Dost thou in conscience think, – tell me, Emilia, –
	That there be women do abuse their husbands
	In such gross kind?
Emil.	There be some such, no question.
Des.	Wouldst thou do such a deed, for all the world?
Emil.	Why, would not you?
Des.	No, by this heavenly light!
Emil.	Nor I neither, by this heavenly light,
	I might do it as well in the dark.
Des.	Wouldst thou do such a thing for all the world?
Emil.	The world is a huge thing, it is a great price,
	For a small vice.
	. . .
Des.	Beshrew me, if I would do such a wrong,
	For the whole world. (IV.iii.60–78)

Emilia then makes an extended, sensible statement about marital responsibility and the behaviour of husbands and wives, without affecting Desdemona's view. In a world that is less than ideal, people of such noble idealism as Othello and Desdemona must come to grief.

Othello as a Problem Play

A downfall based on the incompatibility of idealism with harsh reality might perhaps be judged aesthetically *appropriate*, but not necessary – necessity is a matter of plot. And it is in the working out of the plot that *Othello* can be seen to be lacking necessity and to be similar to the Problem Plays. Unlike many of the plays which have a quality of naturalism, whereby actions are carried out which the audience witness and respond to as if they occurred without the intervention of the playwright – as it were, 'naturally' – the events of the Problem Plays and audience responses to them are more clearly 'staged'. They are manipulated in such a way as to force the audience into sets of responses that contradict each other (this is briefly discussed in the Introduction in regard to *All's Well that Ends Well*).

The nobility of Othello inspires admiration, but at the same time both he and Desdemona irritate by being foolish: why does Othello credit Iago so readily? why does he not confront Desdemona? why does Desdemona not question Othello on his

seething but inarticulate anger before the murder scene? Even if
critics can supply answers to some of these questions, often they
can do so only by invoking material beyond what is seen in the
play. A realistic logic does not work.

Iago's plot is the masterpiece of manipulation. It certainly
works on stage but, only a moment out of the scene, its logic
appears ridiculous. The technique of persuasion used is reminiscent of a scene in the much earlier *Richard III*, where Richard
courts Lady Anne. There, in fewer than 200 lines, Richard
becomes engaged to the woman whose husband and father-in-
law he is known to have slain only a short time before.
Dramatically it works but, at the same time, seems like a trick.
Iago's poisoning of Othello's mind, which is accomplished over
the space of some 450 lines, similarly seems a trick – a brilliant
proof which, while seemingly it cannot be faulted, yet does not
quite feel adequate to the reality. It is 'stage logic', like the solid
look of the two-dimensional movie set.

The strongest element of Iago's 'proof' has nothing to do
with forensic logic but with the attack on Othello's vision, his
idealistic view of humanity. Othello recognises early on that Iago
is playing with rhetorical techniques – 'By heaven, he echoes
me,/ As if there were some monster in his thought' (III.iii.110–
11) – but he cannot withstand the revulsion of Iago's presentation of sexual relationships. 'Goats and monkeys', bestial sexuality, is the image Iago presents. He asks Othello if he wants to
watch Desdemona and Cassio having sex, and says it is too
difficult to arrange:

> Were they as prime as goats, as hot as monkeys,
> As salt as wolves, in pride; and fools as gross
> As ignorance made drunk; but yet I say,
> If imputation and strong circumstances . . .
> (III.iii.409–12)

This is the rhetorical trick of hypothetical statement that functions as if it were an actuality; i.e., Othello has to *think* the picture
of what Iago says in order to follow the conversation, and the
thought of what is hypothetical is realised in the mind with the
same concreteness as the thought of the actuality. Iago in effect is

destroying Othello's vision, and eventually Othello utters 'goats and monkeys' on his own, to Ludovico (IV.i.259).

Virtue is merely image for Iago; the plot, as he formulated it in Act II, scene iii, is about that image:

> So will I turn her virtue into pitch,
> And out of her own goodness make the net
> That shall enmesh 'em all. (II.iii.351–3)

'Her honour is an essence that's not seen' (IV.i.16) Iago tells Othello; having destroyed the image, he has destroyed the thing. This is not like Laertes's honour – an abstract code that he must fulfil to be honourable – but an image of the value of humanity, a relationship that makes both of them meaningful as human beings. Othello is setting out to punish, not a violation committed by Desdemona, but a destruction of an ideal of humanity, an injury that goes beyond codes, that is as insufferable as Lear's torments. Othello says it is not the adulterous sex he cares about but the destruction of a relationship, a vision of himself and the world that depends on the image of Desdemona and their relationship:

> I had been happy if the general camp,
> Pioners, and all, had tasted her sweet body,
> So I had nothing known: O now for ever
> Farewell the tranquil mind, farewell content:
> Farewell the plumed troop, and the big wars,
> That makes ambition virtue: O farewell,
> . . .
> Farewell, Othello's occupation's gone!
> (III.iii.351–63)

And when he comes to kill her in Act V, scene ii, he says 'Yet she must die, else she'll betray more men' (V.ii.6), suggesting that the cause, however personally felt, is not just personal: Desdemona, as imagined by Othello, is a threat to an ideal world, capable of killing a vision broader than just his own, and therefore she must die.

The destruction of the virtuous image of the world is not done exclusively through a sense of sexual disgust; part of the problem of Iago is that he cannot recognise anything that is not material, like honour, and pays inordinate attention to what is (to use an oxymoron) most essentially material, money. Thus his lecture to Roderigo on his pursuit of Desdemona is fundamentally advising him to 'put money in thy purse', five times more reiterated in the same speech (I.iii.335–62). The materialism is thus connected to concerns that go beyond Iago; Iago becomes a figure whose own personal motivation is less important than the attitudes he represents. These attitudes do not require in the drama any explanation of their origin. We do not need to know why or how Iago came to these views in order for the play to be successful; it is sufficient that they are seen as typical of the world from which they come.

The emphasis on materialism, and the individualism of which Iago is also a representative, is thematically consistent with Shakespeare's concerns in the other tragedies, and in some ways *Othello* can be seen as a prototype for *King Lear*. Coming only one or two years earlier, it displays in more stylised form many of the specific elements that enter into *Lear*. Thus the problem of where the duty of the child is owed is raised by Brabantio in the Senate, in a manner parallel to that of Lear, and he receives from Desdemona an answer much like that of Cordelia (I.iii.178–89), and with a result similar to her banishment. Iago strongly resembles Edmund in many particulars, and some of his speeches take their final shape in Edmund's utterance. For example:

> Virtue? a fig! 'tis in ourselves, that we are thus, or thus: our bodies are gardens, to the which our wills are gardeners . . . either to have it sterile with idleness, or manur'd with industry, why, the power, and corrigible authority of this, lies in our wills. (I.iii.319–26)

This is a prototype of Edmund's 'bastard' speech. The individualism of his money lecture to Roderigo – that his purpose is simply to satisfy his will – introduces a note which, again, reverberates more forcefully in Edmund. Cassio's innocence, which is not a naivety but a positive and therefore trusting attitude toward people, makes him a parallel to Edgar, and the way Iago treats him reinforces his similarity to Edmund.

In the same way that *King John* introduces in a crude form concepts that become embodied in incident in the *Henry IV* plays (e.g., 'That smooth-fac'd gentleman, tickling commodity' – II.i.573), so *Othello* introduces much of the material that becomes organised experience in *King Lear*.

Yet *Othello* is clearly not just a prototype of *Lear*. While it may advance concepts that achieve clarity in the later play, it is unsettling in a very different manner. Othello's murder of Desdemona is not just sad; it is stupid. It was recognised by Othello as a mistake and certainly has no tragic necessity. And in this *Othello* is quite different from the other tragedies. The downfall of the usual hero is based on admirable qualities – that is what makes it tragic; Othello's is based on ignorance, admirable only to the limited extent that it stems from a twisted application of his noble idealism but is essentially stupid. There is no way that the problems in *Hamlet* or *Macbeth* or *King Lear* could be resolved or the catastrophe averted by more *information*; their conflicts were fundamental, part of the very structure of the play. But if Othello knew more, only a little bit more, the tragedy would have been prevented. More than unnecessary, the catastrophe is frivolous; yet it is serious and moving. Shakespeare teases the audience, making them produce a tragic emotional response to a mechanical problem. This can be irritating for an audience: they are cheated of a worthy ending when they have been led to expect catharsis.

Othello works on the audience in the same way as *Troilus and Cressida*, *All's Well that Ends Well* and *Measure for Measure*. The audience is led to admire a noble vision in the play and then that vision is ridiculed. We are made to feel slightly foolish for admiring something so insubstantial and so easily destroyed. The other tragedies (except *Coriolanus* and *Timon*), even in the destruction of the heroes, confirm a positive vision of mankind; *Othello*, like the problem plays, offers accident and mockery. The destruction of Othello feels strangely akin to Pandarus's epilogue in *Troilus and Cressida* – we are subjected to, not just witnessing, the hostility of the play. *Othello* is a Problem Tragedy.

INDEX